STUDIES IN EUROPEAN HISTORY

IV

THE LIFE OF
THOMAS HOWARD

EARL OF SURREY AND
SECOND DUKE OF NORFOLK

1443-1524

by

MELVIN J. TUCKER

1964

MOUTON & CO

LONDON · THE HAGUE · PARIS

Printed in The Netherlands by Mouton & Co., Printers, The Hague

TO

W.R. AND N.E.T.

IN GRATEFUL APPRECIATION

FOR

THEIR ENCOURAGEMENT AND HELP

PREFACE

Biography emphasizes, as does no other study, the unique events that collectively make up a particular man's existence. It has the virtue of making history more vivid through the analysis of one man's life. The problems of historical cause, free will, and chance when reduced to the singular, carry a personal, concrete message to the reader which is sometimes lacking in the histories of institutions and group action. Man's wonder and appreciation of his fellow man's tragic dilemmas, individual shortcomings, and modest achievements are enhanced by the successful biography. Though too often biographers are led into the error of making sweeping generalizations on the basis of limited information, the biographer has the moral responsibility of fusing the unique elements in the life of his historical character into the general pattern of historical development as he sees it. Without the unique there can be little interest in the intrinsic worth of the individual or any basis for seeing the characteristics which set one man apart from another; and without the general, the life of the individual has no relevance. Obviously, unique events must be melded and blended into general patterns until the essential meaning hidden in a man's life is apparent. This present study is an attempt to explain what was unique in the life of Thomas Howard, earl of Surrey and second duke of Norfolk, 1443-1524, and what was relevant in it to England's political developments. This, then, is a political biography of a man who lived in the waning days of the fifteenth century and the early part of the sixteenth. The duke was born at a time when a strong council governed a weak king, Henry VI; yet he lived to see the fulfillment of a process to which he himself contributed: the existence of a strong monarchy under Henry VII who ruled his council and tamed his nobility. Though not born to the purple, Howard ended his days as one of two dukes in the realm. He was a new noble in Yorkist days, having been created Earl of Surrey by Richard III, but when he

died, his children considered themselves members of the old aris-
tocracy. His life demonstrates the way in which rising gentry push
their way to the top of the social scale. Of course, political sagacity,
good marriages, fortunate accidents, and proximity to the king, the
usual marks of the gentry's successful advance to higher status, are
all contained in his exciting story.

As a story, Howard's life has the intrinsic interest of all biography.
His career is a study of the steadfast man, of the man loyal to his
king and to his own guiding principle of enlightened self-interest.
Fortunately for Thomas Howard, he always found that he could
gratify the latter by serving the former. He did not make the mistake
of putting service to self above duty to his sovereign. If his own
caution and cleverness were not enough to convince him that this was
the wisest policy, the executions of William Stanley in 1495 and
Edward Stafford, duke of Buckingham, in 1521 were grim reminders
that treason seldom paid. Even with the greatest amount of circum-
spection it was still possible to come dangerously close to losing one's
head on Tower Hill. Howard knew intimately the inside of the Tower
keep, where he had been confined by Henry VII for fighting on the
losing side at Bosworth Field.

In a way, Thomas Howard was a man who spent his life in the
shadow of greater historical figures. Consider these examples: his
father, John Howard, who first established the Howards as one of the
leading noble families; Richard III, who made valuable use of Thomas's
talents as his steward; Henry VII, who entrusted him with the offices
of Lieutenant of the North and Treasurer General; Henry VIII, who
depended upon him as a councillor and diplomat; and Thomas Wolsey,
Henry VIII's chancellor, who dominated him. There is a certain
virtue in studying men who are overshadowed by others. If one can
measure the length of the shadow, one can estimate the size of the
tree; thus, the lives of the great men with whom Thomas Howard
came into contact will be illuminated as well as Howard's. His relationship with his king is a particularly fruitful field of inquiry, for it
reveals something about the character of the four different kings he
served and the nature of kingship in the declining middle ages. One
major theme manifests itself as the evidence is gathered, colated, and
interpreted: the personal responsibility of each king for the running
of his government and for the personal fortunes of his noblemen. Out
of this study of Thomas Howard's relationship with the kings, a body
of evidence has been amassed which shows that he was a far more

important councillor than previous historians have suspected. His duties as steward for Richard III, as Lieutenant of the North for Henry VII, and Treasurer of England for both Henry VII and Henry VIII point this up.

His life, too, is not without drama. Hardly any major English battle between 1470 and 1514 was fought without him being present as a knight or as a military commander. Both his greatest triumph and his greatest personal tragedy were found on the battlefield. His victory at Flodden in 1513 brought him the dukedom of Norfolk, while his defeat at Bosworth led to his imprisonment. There is also mystery in his involvement with Richard III and the murder of the little princes. Who else but the Howards, other than Richard, gained so much from their deaths? In addition, his personal intrigue to control Henry VIII's council marks an important chapter in his life.

Though the primary emphasis in this biography is political, certain constitutional aspects of Howard's tenure as Lieutenant of the North under Henry VII and Treasurer General under both Henry VII and Henry VIII have been examined. The usual image of Howard as a tired nobleman performing inconsequential duties on state occasions has been dispelled. Though the Treasurer General only very rarely handled finances, he was the administrative head of a powerful organization and by virtue of his office was a member of that trio of royal officers: the treasurer, chancellor, and privy seal, which acted as an executive committee for the king's council. Moreover, Howard was involved in much of his country's diplomacy and was actively engaged, at different times in his career, in negotiating peace treaties, truces, and marriage alliances with Scotland, France, and Spain. He was also interested in the arts and as such, a patron of the poet, Alexander Barclay, and it might be added that his first wife, Elizabeth Tylney, was patroness to John Skelton, the Tudor poet.

No attempt has been made to exhaust the unlimited resources of the Public Record Office. However, for Howard's career as Lieutenant of the North, use has been made of pertinent patents, the Tellers Rolls, and the Ministers Accounts for the royal lordship of Sheriff Hutton. Manuscripts located in the British Museum and the Bodleian, have also been used. In addition, the author has consulted the principal sources in print, the necessary secondary works, and local record publications.

It is a pleasure to record the many obligations I have incurred during the preparation of this book. I am very grateful to Professor

Lacey B. Smith for his constant encouragement, his helpful criticism, and his friendship. To Professor Gray C. Boyce I am indebted for advice on the study of medieval Latin and aid given in obtaining a vital manuscript; to Professor S. T. Bindoff I owe a special debt of gratitude for aid and counsel while I was in England; and to Professor Francis C. Wormald go my thanks for introducing me to the study of English paleography. The following have also been helpful: Mr. F. C. Emmison of the Essex Record Office, Miss Mary R. McGuinness of the Staff of the York Public Library, Miss Doris Coates of the National Register of Archives, Mr. S. J. Arthur of the Manuscript Room in the British Museum, Mrs. Gladys Cowles, Miss Susan Flower, Miss Helen Miller, Professor T. G. Barnes, Mr. Keith Wallis, and Mr. E. K. Timming of the Public Record Office. In addition, I must record my indebtedness to the Commission for International Education which made possible a year's study in England, and to the American Philosophical Society for a grant-in-aid. Oliver and Boyd Publishers, Ltd. have kindly allowed me to reproduce a combination map and battle plan of Flodden from R. L. Mackie, *King James IV of Scotland: A Brief Survey of His Life and Times* (London, 1958). I am similarly obligated to the D. Appleton-Century-Crofts Company for permission to use portraits of John Howard, first duke of Norfolk, and of Thomas Howard from Gerald Brenan and Edward Phillips Statham, *The House of Howard*, 2 vols. (New York, 1908). His Grace, the Duke of Norfolk, has generously permitted the reproduction of the portrait of Thomas Howard, duke of Norfolk.

I am deeply grateful to the Committee on Publications of the State University of New York at Buffalo which has provided a generous subvention towards the publication of this book.

Buffalo, New York   Melvin J. Tucker
December, 1963

TABLE OF CONTENTS

ILLUSTRATIONS

ABBREVIATIONS

A. H. R.	*American Historical Review*
B. M.	British Museum
Bull. Instit. Hist. Research	*Bulletin of the Institute of Historical Research*
C. C. R.	*Calendar of the Close Rolls*
C. D. R. Scot.	*Calendar of the Documents Relating to Scotland*
C. I. P. M. H VII	*Calendar of the Inquisitions Post Mortem of Henry VII*
C. S. P.	*Calendar of the State Papers:* used with the abbreviations *Span.* for *Spanish* and *Ven.* for *Venetian*
D. N. B.	*Dictionary of National Biography*
E. E. T. S.	Early English Text Society
E. H. R.	*English Historical Review*
G. E. C.	*The Complete Peerage*
Gents. Mag.	*Gentleman's Magazine*
J. H. L.	*Journal of the House of Lords*
L. P.	*Letters and Papers*
L. P. R III & H VII	*Letters and Papers of Richard III and Henry VII*
N. E. D.	*New English Dictionary*
P. R. O.	Public Record Office, London
Rot. Parl.	*Rotuli Parliamentorum*
Rot. Scot.	*Rotuli Scotiae*

References to *C. C. R., C. D. R. Scot., C. I. P. M. H VII, C. S. P. Milan, C. S. P. Span., C. S. P. Ven.,* and *L. P.* are to document numbers and not to pages. The 1920 Brodie edition of volume one of *L. P.* has been used and not that prepared by Brewer. Bibliographical particulars are presented in the bibliography on pp. 145-151.

I

YOUTH AND EARLY MANHOOD

Many a man's fate has been decided by the outcome of a battle, and the fifteenth century witnessed many dramatic reversals of fortune as a result of the battles fought in the Wars of the Roses. None was more astonishing than Henry Tudor's emergence from Bosworth Field as a king, or Thomas Howard's decline and imprisonment for having supported Richard III in this same engagement. Before Bosworth, the Howard star had been in the ascendant: King Richard had rewarded Thomas's father, John, by creating him Duke of Norfolk, granting him innumerable properties, and utilizing him as his chief admiral and general. The son, no less than the father, had received special marks of the royal favor and had been made Earl of Surrey and given a handsome annuity. But the Howards, a *nouveau riche* family that had only achieved nobility within John's lifetime, were so firmly attached to Richard's coattails that they shared in his failure as well as his success. Thus, their king's defeat and death at Bosworth had important consequences for them. John lost his life fighting in the vanguard of Richard's forces, while his son, gravely wounded, was borne off the field in a litter under close arrest. Thomas Howard faced an uncertain future. Though he was not immediately put to death like Catesby, one of Richard's staunchest followers, he could expect little from his conqueror. His position as steward of Richard's household made him a marked man: he would be lucky to save his life. He was imprisoned in the Tower of London and while there was attainted by Henry's first parliament. By this act of attainder he lost all honors, titles, and lands. Though he received a pardon from the new king in the following year, it was stipulated that the former earl was to be imprisoned during the king's pleasure. The phenomenal rise of the Howard family to a position of affluence and political prominence appeared at an end, but in fact, it had merely experienced a temporary setback.

That Howard lived to fight another day is as much a testament to Henry's generosity as it is to the first Tudor's regard for and need of the earl's unique talents. When Henry had assured himself of Howard's loyalty, he employed him as his Lieutenant of the North in protecting the border counties against the depredations of the hostile Scots and in crushing the northern rebellions and riots that plagued the house of Tudor. The earl kept order in the North and as a reward for his services he was made Treasurer General. As such, he was administrative head of the exchequer and had authority to appoint some of its officers and control the customs service. Though both Henry VII and Henry VIII used Howard as treasurer, councillor, and even as a diplomat, it was as a general that he became famous. There are few English schoolboys who do not today recognize the Earl of Surrey as the victor at Flodden Field where on September 9, 1513 his forces completely defeated, demoralized, and routed the Scots who left many of their countrymen lying dead on the bloody moor, including their brave king, James IV. The earl's victory was the means of his advancement to the dukedom of Norfolk and of obtaining a sizeable grant in lands from Henry VIII.

From the time of his release from confinement in 1489 to his death in 1524, Howard's story records the service of an efficient councillor, an energetic diplomat, and a brilliant general who became one of the most powerful men in the realm. Not only was the duke an important political figure, but he was also at the top of the social order, since he and Charles Brandon, the duke of Suffolk and the king's brother-in-law, were the only English dukes. Howard's political and social position enabled him to provide his children with suitable husbands and wives, so that the Howard family was connected to most of the important English nobility. This is a brief sketch of the life of Thomas Howard, earl of Surrey and second duke of Norfolk.

Thomas Howard was born in 1443, the eldest son of John and Catherine Moleyns Howard.[1] Until the middle of the fifteenth century the Howards had been small landowners of some consequence in either Suffolk or Norfolk, and if the career of Thomas's father, John, is any indication, they were also involved in commercial enterprises. They were typical of the fairly well-to-do English gentry who wanted to get on in the world by building up large estates and by marrying beyond their station. Back in the dim past they could claim among

---

[1] John Weever, *Antient Funeral Monuments* ... (London, 1631), p. 839. Hereafter cited as Weever. See also *C. S. P. Ven.*, II, 219.

their ancestors one Sir William Howard who was Chief Justice of Common Pleas during the reigns of Edward I and Edward II. Save for this gentleman and an occasional Howard who rose to the eminence of admiral of the King's fleet, the family influence was confined primarily to local as opposed to national interests. Later Howards, born in the sixteenth century, would claim the redoubtable Saxon Hereward, the antagonist of William the Conqueror, as the founder of their line, but this was wishful thinking on their part and the fabrication of clever heralds.[2]

Actually, the Howard fortunes were made by a fortunate marriage. Thomas's grandfather, Robert, married Margaret Mowbray, the daughter of Thomas Mowbray, duke of Norfolk and Lord Segrave and Mowbray. When the Mowbray line became extinct in 1481, John Howard, Thomas's father, became one of the co-heirs to the vast Mowbray properties. Through this marriage, future Howards inherited the blood of kings, for Margaret was descended from Thomas Brotherton, a son of Edward I and so could claim the earlier English kings as ancestors.[3] This marriage prepared the way for the Howard ascent to the dukedom of Norfolk. It was the same old familiar story of petticoat nobility: the older families died off in the male line and were supplanted in their dignities by the husbands or heirs of their daughters.

John Howard was thoroughly immersed in local and court politics, engaged in commercial activity, and involved in the most important military campaigns of his day. He was born just in time to participate in the Hundred Years War. He fought at Chatillon in July 1453 and had the misfortune to be taken prisoner.[4] Even as Howard fought in this engagement, it was apparent that the English had little hope of holding on to their rapidly diminishing lands in France. With the appearance of Joan of Arc in 1429 and the crowning of Charles VII

---

[2] Arthur Collins, *The Peerage Of England* . . . , 2nd ed., 5 vols. (1741-56), I, 6-7. Hereafter cited as Collins. Henry Howard thought the Howards took a Saxon name since they were originally of Saxon descent. Henry Howard, *Indication of Memorials, Monuments, Paintings, and Engravings of Persons of the Howard Family* . . . (Corbey Castle, 1834), Appendix I, and p. 1 of the text. Hereafter cited as *Memorials*. See also J. Horace Round, *Studies in Peerage And Family History* (Westminster, 1901), p. 75. Hereafter cited as Round.

[3] *Ibid.*, pp. 435-46. Also see Table I on page 16.

[4] Collins, I, 8; James Dallaway and Edmund Cartwright, *A History Of The Western Division Of The County Of Sussex* . . . , 2 vols. (London, 1815-32), II, pt. 2, 188. Hereafter cited as Dallaway. John Howard was born between 1420 and 1422, probably at Tendring Hall in Stoke-Nayland. *Memorials*, p. 7.

TABLE I

The Howard and Mowbray Genealogy [a]

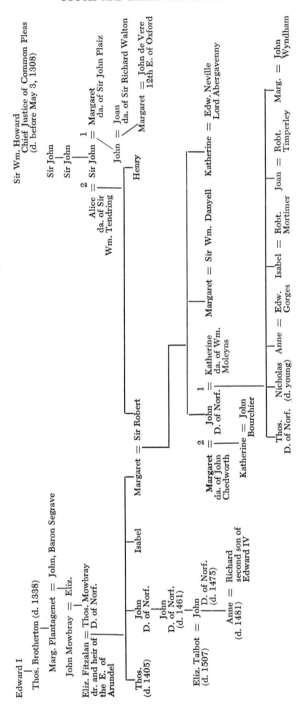

a   Burke's Peerage, pp. 1674-75; *D.N.B.*, X, 44; *G.E.C.*, IX, 596-610; Turner, "Introduction", p. xc.

of France, the tide had begun to turn against the English. Gradually they were forced from province after province until only the city of Calais remained when the two countries ceased hostilities in 1453. Because of the English losses, English Francophobia intensified, and the traditional English anti-French policy became even more firmly entrenched in the minds of the English. Dreams of Henry V's triumphs did not die easily. For the next hundred years English kings sought to revive and realize their claims to the French throne. Thus, they punctuated their hate for France with sporadic raids, massive attacks, and periodic truces. It was not until the days of Elizabeth that Spain replaced France as the traditional enemy, and this diplomatic *volte-face* was dictated by national rather than feudal interests.

Upon his release as a hostage in France, John Howard plunged into local politics. He stood for election as an M.P. for Norfolk in 1455. Here his connection with his first cousin, John Mowbray, duke of Norfolk, stood him in good stead and much to the disgust of the local notables, Howard's candidacy was advanced by the duke. Prior to the election, the duchess of Norfolk wrote to John Paston, a member of the Norfolk gentry and an important landholder, requesting his support for her husband's choices for the parliamentary seats, Howard and Sir Roger Chamberlain. She made it quite clear to Paston that it is ". . . right necessarie for divers causes that my Lord have at this tyme in the Parlement suche persones as longe unto him, and be of his menyall servaunts, wherin we conceyve your good will and diligence shal be right expedient, we hertili desire and pray you that at the contemplacion of thise oure lettres, as our special trust is in you, ye wil geve and applie your voice unto our right welbelovid cosin and servaunts, John Howard and Syr Roger Chambirlayn, to be Knyghts of the shire, exorting all such othir as be your wisdom shal now be behovefull, to the good exployte and conclusion of the same."[5]

Receipt of this letter must have been especially galling and disappointing to Paston who wanted the office for himself. Paston had solid popular support for his candidacy while Howard, whose lands were in Suffolk, was considered an outsider. John Jenney, a man sent out by the Duke of Norfolk to stimulate acceptance of Howard as a candidate, ran into considerable local opposition. He reported to Paston that he had ". . . tolde my Lord of Norffolk atte London that I

---

[5] James Gairdner (ed.), *The Paston Letters A. D. 1422-1509*, 6 vols. (London, 1904), III, 34. Hereafter cited as *Paston Letters*.

labored diverse men for Sir Roger Chaumberleyn, and they seid to me they wolde have hym, but not Howard, in asmeche as he hadde no lyvelode in the shire, nor conversement [i.e. acquaintance?]; and I asked them hom they wolde have, and they seid they wolde have you, and thus I tolde hym. And he seid on avysely, as he kan doo full well, I myght not sey ye labored ther, for I herde never sey ye labored therfor, be the feithe I vowe to God."[6] The duke was so concerned about the election that he became willing to yield in the matter of his cousin's candidacy. He agreed that it might be possible to allow a free election as long as the shire did not elect Sir Thomas Todenham or any candidate favorable to John de la Pole, the duke of Suffolk. When John Howard heard this he "... was as wode as a wilde bullok..."[7] But John Howard was wroth for nothing, he was elected — his cousin's influence had prevailed.

Men of the shire might grumble about Howard's election and show their resentment passively, but few thought about taking any definite action. They knew only too well the extent of the Duke of Norfolk's powers. In his own area the duke's power was supreme. With the help of his council he determined local affairs and influenced causes handled in his courts. The power of the local magnate was enhanced and increased by the weakness of the crown. Lack of governance and lack of a strong central authority also contributed to the anarchical conditions in the shires. Who was to prevent each magnate from managing affairs in his locality to suit his taste? Generally, the magnates had their way — except when they came into conflict with one another. And the numerous feuds among the magnates also caused anarchy.

The country was weakened by a long regency during Henry VI's minority. Henry V had died in 1422 at the height of his power and left a son, Henry VI, not quite a year old. The important noble councillors took advantage of the situation to assert their power and struggled with each other to see who should be chief amongst them. The pattern of conciliar domination in affairs of state was set long before Henry VI became king in his own right. When he did attempt to manage his own affairs, he was met by strong conciliar opposition. Being a weak man, he succumbed easily to domination by his council. Moreover, he inherited a touch of insanity from his grandfather, Charles VI, king of France. This insanity made necessary the selection

[6] *Ibid.*, p. 38.
[7] *Ibid.*, p. 39.

in 1454 of Richard Plantagenet, duke of York and father to Edward IV, as Protector of England. Until the birth of a son in 1453 to Henry VI and Queen Margaret, Richard was not only duke of York, but also the heir apparent to the English throne. The birth of Edward, Henry VI's son, on October 13, 1453 changed the duke's status. Henry's recovery of his reason early in 1455 made the duke of York's duties as Protector unnecessary; but the duke and his intimates did not relish relinquishing their authority to Henry and the Lancastrian faction. Thus, the basis for the Wars of the Roses was laid in Richard's taste for power, Henry VI's weakness and insanity, the prevalent factionalism existant in the king's council, and the general realization that if events followed their natural course, Richard of York had little hope of becoming king.

The end of hostilities in France freed soldiers for military operations in England. Each side, Lancastrian and Yorkist, filled their ranks with the numerous professional soldiers now free to serve with new military masters. From following the pursuit of profit and booty in France, these men turned eagerly to the pursuit of gain through following one of the factions. The Wars of Roses were primarily factional struggles with important lands and the crown of England as prizes. For a man rising in the world of affairs, the battles provided an excellent opportunity to advance himself — providing that he selected the winning side. Fortunately for John Howard, he chose the Yorkist side. Though he was cited in one of Henry VI's commissions to arrest any people who hindered those coming to the king's aid,[8] he paid little attention to this commission. He threw in his lot with Richard Neville, the famous earl of Warwick and staunch supporter of Edward, the new duke of York and Yorkist claimant to the throne. At the battle of Towton on March 29, 1461 he led a contingent of East Anglians into battle and was knighted for his services.[9] His active support of the new Yorkist king, Edward IV, opened to him the floodgates of royal patronage and preferment. He was made Edward's carver, received the office of constable of Colchester Castle, and was appointed sheriff of Norfolk and Suffolk.[10] Except for a quarrel with

---

[8]   C. P. R., 1452-61, p. 656.
[9]   Dallaway, II, pt. 2, 188; James H. Ramsay, *Lancaster and York: A Century Of English History (A. D. 1399-1485)*, 2 vols. (Oxford, 1892), II, 272. Hereafter cited as Ramsay.
[10]   Josiah C. Wedgwood and Anne D. Holt, *History Of Parliament*, 2 vols. (London, 1936-38), I, 473. Wedgwood's work is useful, but opinionated and occasionally in error.

John Paston, a candidate for M.P. for Norfolk, which landed Howard in Fleet Prison for a short sojourn, all went well for Howard in the 1460's.

As sheriff of the counties of Norfolk and Suffolk, Howard made the arrangements for the elections of the M.P.'s. Apparently, he was determined that John Paston should not obtain a parliamentary seat. He wished to prevent Paston's election at any price and he almost succeeded. Paston accused Howard of instigating a brawl in the shire house in which one of Howard's men struck Paston twice with a dagger. According to Howard, however, the fracas technically issued out of a dispute over the limitation of the voting franchise to the forty shilling free holders, but in reality it was caused by Paston's supporters who tried to force him to make a fraudulent return for Paston. Howard declared that he would not be intimidated by these ruffians and swore that he would reveal their riots to the king. Hence, he brought forward a bill against Paston, and as a result of this legal action Paston found himself cast into Fleet prison. But the outcry of the Norfolk people at what they deemed an injustice was so great that an inquiry was held, and there it was determined that Howard, not Paston, was at fault, and so he was put in prison in Paston's place.[11] Many thought that Howard was in serious trouble, and Margaret Paston wrote to her husband John that "... it is told me that Syr John Howard is lek to lese hys hed".[12]

Howard spent some time in the Fleet, but was pardoned on February 6, 1462. He continued to be in favor with the king, for Edward made him constable of Norwich Castle and granted him these lands: Leyham and Wherestede manors, Suffolk; Smethton Hall, Essex; Dontish and Deulish manors in Dorset; Hereford manor and Meyton Hall, Norfolk; and two tenements for his residence in London.[13] He was busy with naval and military matters from 1462 to 1465. In keeping with the English anti-French policy he, along with Lords Say and Clinton, made a raid on the coast of Brittany in 1462. Later that year he fought against the Lancastrians, who still held Alnwich

[11] *Paston Letters*, III, 303, 313-14; IV, 2-5; C. H. Williams, "A Norfolk Parliamentary Election, 1461", *E. H. R.*, XL (1925), 79-86.

[12] *Paston Letters*, IV, 33.

[13] *C. P. R. 1461-67*, pp. 111, 187; *C. C. R. 1461-68*, p. 114. As usual, during the 60's he was on various commissions such as one to inquire into insurrections in Norfolk and Suffolk. He may have served from 1463-65 as an M.P. for Suffolk, and he was on a commission of array for Essex in 1463. *C. P. R. 1461-67*, pp. 277-78, 348; Wedgwood, I. 473.

Fig. 1. John Howard, Duke of Norfolk

Castle, and in 1464 he aided his second cousin, John Mowbray, the new duke of Norfolk, in reducing Wales which had not yet completely accepted the new king.[14]

John Howard's association with his sovereign enabled him to advance his commercial interests. As a shipowner and trader, his close association with Edward IV presented him with unusual business opportunities, such as a special permit to import ten tun of Gascon wine for his household.[15] Richard Outlaw or Richard Felaw, a Walwath and Ipswich merchant, was associated with him in his commercial ventures and acted as his agent, taking Howard's livery in 1465. During the period from 1462-81 Howard was connected with Ipswich and Harwich on the basis of building and supplying ships for Edward IV.[16] Howard, as well as Warwick, the kingmaker, Thomas Neville, Lord Fauconberg and cousin to Warwick, and William Lord Hastings, Edward IV's chamberlain, held export licenses and were involved in extensive trading operations. Howard also shared with John Neville, the earl of Northumberland, the Earl of Warwick, and a George Willerby in a commission for the development of all mines of gold, silver, and lead north of the river Trent.[17] The interest of these important men in commerce and industry is evidence that some of the more important nobles were not afraid to be businessmen. Not all commerce and industry was handled by the middle-class men — the "new men". On the other hand, one must remember that both Hastings and Howard were ennobled by Edward IV. Might one see in Howard's career a parallel to that of William de la Pole, the great Hull merchant and financial advisor to Edward III, whose family acquired the earldom of Suffolk?[18] A king could ennoble whomever he wished, whether the man be a merchant or a country gentleman.

---

[14] Cora L. Scofield, *The Life And Reign Of Edward The Fourth, King of England And of France And Lord Of Ireland*, 2 vols. (London, 1923), I, 249, 258. Hereafter cited as Scofield. *Paston Letters*, IV, 60; Thomas Hudson Turner, ed., "Introduction", *Manners And Household Expenses Of England In The Thirteenth And Fifteenth Centuries Illustrated By Original Records* (London, The Roxburghe Club, 1841), p. lxxxvi. Hereafter cited as Turner.

[15] *Ibid.*, pp. 187, 418.

[16] Eileen Power and M. M. Postan (eds.), *Studies In English Trade In the Fifteenth Century* (London, 1933), 374-378; Winifred I. Haward, "Economic Aspects of the Wars of the Roses in East Anglia", *E. H. R.*, XLI (1926), 181.

[17] *C. P. R. 1467-77*, p. 132. Note also that John Howard was connected to the Nevilles through marriage. His sister Catherine was the second wife to Warwick's uncle, Edward Neville, Lord Abergavenny. Ramsay, II, Table I.

[18] C. L. Kingsford, *Prejudice & Promise in XVth Century England* (Oxford, 1925), p. 146.

John Howard's son, Thomas, on one occasion at least, was taken to Calais on a business trip. While there, during the summer of 1466, Howard bought a quantity of Flemish cloth and other articles which his son itemized in his household book. Both father and son could write and the father was in the habit of keeping his household accounts in his own hand.[19] This practice re-emphasizes John Howard's non-noble background, since most noblemen let their secretaries perform this task.

Actually John Howard had little hope for achieving noble status through his relations to the Mowbray duke of Norfolk. For him to have had any hopes of obtaining the title, or more important, the Mowbray estates, it would have been necessary for the present duke of Norfolk, John Mowbray, to die childless or for his children to die without heirs. This did not seem likely in the 1460's since Mowbray and his wife were still young enough to bear children. Even if the Mowbray duke died without heirs or if he left a daughter who died without heirs, the title did not automatically pass to the heirs of the property. The title would be in abeyance until such time as the king determined that it should be regranted.

In view of his own position as a small landowner and a person engaged in commerce, it seemed to be a good idea to John Howard to send his son to Thetford grammar school. It is not possible to determine how long Thomas attended the grammar school, nor under whom he studied. If he stayed there for any length of time, he would, in due course, have studied Latin, logic, rhetoric, grammar, arithmetic, and probably some music. The prevailing influence in Thomas's education was medieval rather than renaissance. As yet, the new learning had not made a sufficient impression on education in English circles to have filtered down to the grammar school. Most students in his day followed the *quadrivium* and *trivium,* not the new critical scholarship of the Renaissance. They did not learn the profound respect for those ancients and the Greek language which pervaded English universities in the sixteenth century. Their philosophy was not neo-platonic, but scholastic and their guides Scotus and Aquinas,

---

[19]   J. Payne Collier (ed.), "Introduction", *Household Books Of John [Howard], Duke of Norfolk, And Thomas, Earl of Surrey; Temp. 1481-90* (London, Roxburghe Club, 1844), p. xxxix. Hereafter cited as Collier. See also Turner, pp. 366-71. If the entries are in Thomas's hand, and it seems likely, since the first refers to what "my fadir bowt", then John Howard may very well have dictated the entries, since several refer to articles of clothing bought for "my son" and to payment of costs incurred at Calais.

not Plato. As with much education in the dying Middle Ages, for those who were to take a place at the court of nobleman or king, there was an emphasis on chivalry and inculcating in youths those chivalric ideals of honor, loyalty, largess, and courtly love that all professed, but few practiced. Thomas's father's library was a curious mélange of medieval standards such as *Le Miroir de la Mort, La belle Dame sans Merci*; romantic tales like *Ponthus et la belle Sidoyne, Sir Baudin, Conte de Flandres,* and *Le Jeu des Eches,*[20] in which a youth could see clearly charted the formalized structure of decadent chivalry and the way to becoming an agreeable courtier. That Thomas read any or all of these books or that they were in John Howard's possession during Thomas's childhood, can be neither proved nor disproved. What is important, though, is to consider that these books formed a part of the atmosphere in which he lived, an atmosphere of careful respect for chivalric forms gained through a reading of French romances. Thomas must have been conversant with French, which had not yet been wholly supplanted by English as the language of the propertied classes and law courts. Surely his trips to France in 1466, 1471, and 1475 gave him some acquaintance with it.[21]

Neither the art of good manners nor religion were neglected. Dancing was normally taught to youths at the age of ten or twelve,[22] and the influence of the French romances taught a nice regard for the civilities of a cultured life. There was an organ at Tendring Hall, Thomas's birthplace in Suffolk, and at least in a later period the Howard household was often entertained by players and minstrels.[23] Both in manners and in religion scrupulous attention was paid to form and ceremony.

Despite the rigid adherence to prescribed forms of conduct and the emphasis on performing one's duties in a precise way, there was a quantitative rather than qualitative approach to life. This was the reason that such a medievally-oriented monarch as Henry VII

---

[20]   Weever, p. 834; Collier, "Introduction", pp. xxvii-xxix and p. 277 in the text. Thomas and his brother Nicholas's schoolmaster was given a reward of twenty pence on June 6, 1464. Turner, p. 269. It is possible that this schoolmaster resided at Tendring Hall, and if this is so, it would indicate John Howard's rise to affluence during the early years of Edward IV.

[21]   Turner, p. 371; A. R. Myers (ed.), *The Household Of Edward IV: The Black Book And The Ordinance of 1478* (Manchester, 1949), pp. 199, 263. Hereafter cited as Myers.

[22]   Charles Mills, *The History of Chivalry or Knighthood and its times,* 2 vols. (London, 1826), II, 118. Hereafter cited as Mills.

[23]   Collier, "Introduction", p. xxii.

TABLE II

The Tylney Genealogy[a]

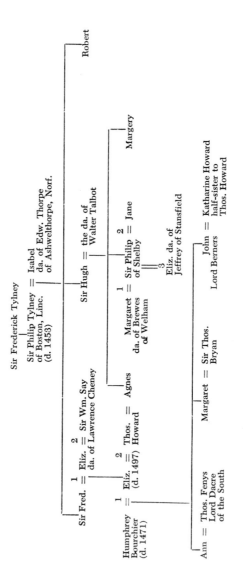

[a] Compiled from B.M. ADD. MS. 19152; John Clay (ed.), *The Visitation of Cambridge* (= *Harleian Society Publications*, XLI (London, 1897), pp. 118-19; *G. E. C.*, IV, 10; *Memorials*, p. 8; *Test. Vet.*, II, 449; *Visitations of Suffolk 1561, 1577, 1612*, ed. W. C. Metcalfe (Exeter, 1882), p. 73.

was not satisfied with merely one or two masses being said for his soul — he had to have ten thousand. Religion clothed both great ceremonies and simple actions with a symbolic meaning. Regard for the religious permeated every facet of life. Thomas was taught at Thetford by clerks, and his education had strong religious and theological overtones. He was not as generous in his religious benefactions as his father, who on one notable occasion contributed to the founding of a chantry,[24] but the religious atmosphere pervaded the fifteenth century, and Thomas could not have been unaffected by it.

Learning manly sports, perfecting chivalric exercises, and training in the art of war were also an integral part of young Thomas's education. Usually, boys began their training in sports of the field at fourteen and jousting at sixteen.[25] The frequent entries in the household accounts for military accoutrements for both Thomas and his younger brother Nicholas attest their familiarity with lances, swords, bows, and coats of mail.[26] Both young men were often together as when they were at Smithfield in March 1464 and at London in April of the same year. Each had a man servant: Thomas's man was John Davy and Nicholas's was Richard Flecher. These men servants' most frequent errand seemed to be the task of bringing money from home to their young masters.[27] After taking part in 1469 in a naval expedition with Anthony, Lord Scales, little more is heard of Nicholas Howard. He disappears from view, and one can probably infer that he died young either from disease or in battle.[28] Death had also claimed Thomas's mother Catherine in November 1465. She had been ill in September, for we find three separate items in the household accounts for the twenty-first of September dealing with her medicines and with the cost of John Clerke for looking after her. She died on the thirteenth of November 1465 and Thomas, Nicholas, and their sister, Isabel, were each given three yards of black cloth for mourning, while the other Howard children were given lesser amounts. Within a year and a half John Howard remarried, marrying Margaret, the daughter

---

[24] *C. P. R. 1467-1477*, p. 484. The fact that Thomas does not seem to have made as many benefactions as John Howard may be due to scarcity of records and not that one was more religious or generous than the other.

[25] Mills, II, 118.

[26] Turner, pp. 356, 361, 567-69.

[27] *Ibid.*, pp. 256-57, 416, 568, 607. Other servants who brought money to the two youths were William Fernwale, Thomas Thorpe, and a man named Seynclow [Sinclair]. *Ibid.*, pp. 256-57, 419, 426.

[28] *Ibid.*, 567-68; Ramsay, II, 334-35.

TABLE III

The Children of Thomas Howard[a]

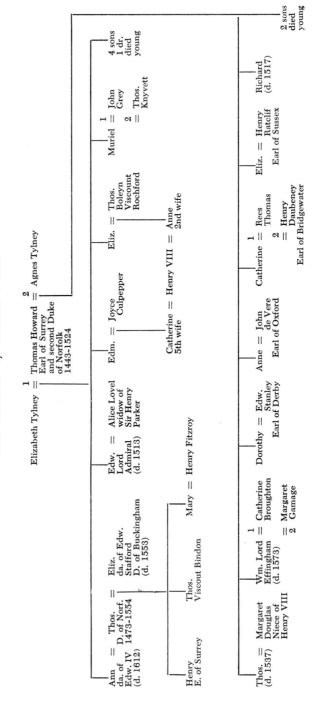

[a]   *Memorials*, pp. 11-15, 87-88.

of Sir John Chedworth, in January 1467 and by her he had one daughter — who married John, Lord Berners, the translator of Froissart.[29]

Shortly after the death of his mother, Thomas entered the service of King Edward as a henchman. A henchman's duties were chiefly ceremonial: it was his duty to assist great men or women, usually princes or princesses, when they participated in state processions and progresses. Under Edward IV and Richard III, the number of royal henchmen was limited to seven and these seven were placed under the command of the master of the horse.[30] Thomas probably entered into his new duties sometime in 1466. There is a record in this year of money taken to him at Windsor and subsequent gifts delivered there and at London and Salisbury in 1467, 1468, and 1469. He was with the king at Salisbury on January 11, 1469;[31] thus, he was present when Edward IV was being harried from the land by Warwick and George, duke of Clarence, Edward IV's brother. Thomas did not escape with Edward IV to the Low Countries; instead, he took sanctuary at the church of Saint Joan's in Colchester.[32]

The spectacle of Edward's chief supporter, Richard Neville, the earl of Warwick, and the king's own brother, George, duke of Clarence, turning against their sovereign is surprising to one unfamiliar with fifteenth century politics. Edward IV owed his throne to the strong support given him by Neville and his retainers. In return for his aid, Warwick, the kingmaker, expected to manipulate English affairs to suit himself. Warwick favored peace with France and hoped to cement an Anglo-French accord with a royal marriage. He wanted Edward IV to marry Bona of Savoy, a sister to the queen of France. The new French king, Louis XI, who had ascended the French throne in 1461, was enthusiastic about this alliance, for he saw the possibility of ending the costly wars with England and the consequent freeing of his military and economic resources for use in his struggle with Burgundy. Warwick was the chief English negotiator, and he became quite friendly with the wily Louis XI. Imagine Warwick's chagrin when in September 1464 he learned of Edward's secret marriage in the previous month of May to the attractive Elizabeth Woodville, the

[29] Turner, "Introduction", p. lxxxvi, xc, and pp. 304, 384, 582. See also *Paston Letters*, IV, 211-13.
[30] *N. E. D.*, V, 221.
[31] Turner, pp. 369, 416, 426, 529-30.
[32] Ramsay, II. 342-57; Weever, p. 834.

widow of Sir John Grey. Not only was Elizabeth the widow of a Lancastrian supporter, but she brought to court her father, two sons, five brothers, and seven sisters. Of course, she expected her husband to provide handsomely for each relative. Thus, Warwick's foreign policy evaporated, and he was in danger of being supplanted in Edward's councils by the Woodville interest. Warwick's disaffection grew steadily, and he did not attend the new queen's coronation in May 1465. An Anglo-Burgundian alliance based on the marriage of Edward's sister Margaret to Charles the Bold of Burgundy was substituted for Warwick's proposed alliance with France. And Warwick's brother George Neville, the archbishop of Canterbury and the chancellor of England, lost his post as chancellor.

Warwick's displeasure was evident. Though he and the duke of Clarence did not actually rebel until 1469,[33] he must have been formulating his plans long before. John Howard had connections with both men: he had taken Clarence's livery on August 5, 1465 and a year later took Warwick's.[34] Whether or not he seriously entertained thoughts of supporting them is an interesting but unanswerable question. He had been amply rewarded by Edward for his services and the king continued to entrust him with important commissions, such as the working out of the Anglo-Burgundian alliance and service as one of the escorts to Edward's sister Margaret on her trip to Burgundy. In 1467 he had been made treasurer of the royal household, and in one royal commission dated that year he was styled Lord Howard. Thus, he was probably ennobled by Edward IV sometime during 1467, since he received individual writs for all subsequent parliaments.[35]

Both Thomas and his father supported Edward against Warwick, who had succeeded in placing Henry VI on the English throne and maintained him there from October 1470 to May 1471. When Edward returned to England, John Howard proclaimed him king in the county of Suffolk, and fought for him at the battles of Tewkesbury and Barnet where his son was wounded.[36] This battle was also notable for the

---

[33] Ramsay, II, 306-37; Scofield, I, 343-54.
[34] Turner, pp. 299, 365.
[35] Scofield, I, 410; Wedgwood, I, 473-74; Dallaway, II, pt. 2, 189; *Memorials*, Appendix IV. John Howard was also a knight for the shire of Suffolk in 1467 and spent over forty pounds feasting his electors. He also served on a number of commissions of the peace and commissions of array during this period. *D. N. B.*, X, 42-43; *C. P. R.*, 1461-67, pp. 559, 568-73.
[36] Wedgwood, I, 474; Weever, p. 834; Ramsay, II, 371.

defeat and death of Warwick, who had failed in his original attempt to put Clarence on the throne. Clarence had married Warwick's eldest daughter, Isabel, and he was Warwick's candidate for the throne until he proved neither courageous nor pliable enough to suit Warwick's taste. In fact, Clarence became reconciled to his brother before Warwick's plans could fully mature. It was then that Warwick entertained the idea of putting Henry VI back on the English throne. To facilitate this second undertaking, Warwick's second daughter, Anne, was betrothed to Edward, Henry VI's heir and Warwick launched his successful military invasion of England. Eventually, both Warwick and his new son-in-law lost their lives defending Henri VI's right to the English crown.[37]

Edward IV's victory meant a great deal to both Howards. For the elder Howard it meant service as deputy governor in Calais, and for Thomas, service as esquire to the king's body.[38] Esquires of the body were the king's attendants who bore the various articles of the king's armor, such as his lance and shield. During Edward's time there were at least forty knights and esquires who served in the household and out of these, four were selected to be of the body. Two of these waited quarterly on the king, while the other two were not in attendance; only one was on duty at a time except in processions. They were under the lord chamberlain's jurisdiction, performed their duties in the rooms above the stairs, and generally were gentlemen of birth or good alliance. Among their duties were: making ready the king's cupboard at night, assisting a gentleman usher in the supervision of the making of the king's bed, helping the king in his toilet, serving the king his pottage at dinner and supper, and taking charge of the house above and below the stairs during the night.[39] As one can see, the job involved constant personal contact with the king and was one of the most responsible positions of any entrusted to those who waited on the king. Thomas probably began his stint as an esquire-to-the-body in October of 1471, for his epitaph states that: ". . . when he was at mannes age, was wyth dyuers other Gentlemen of Englond, sent to Charles, Duke of Burgon, in the begynnyng of the warres betwixt kynge Lewes of Fraunce, and the seid Duke Charles, and ther contynued unto thende of the seid warres, to hys greate prayse and

---

[37] Ibid., pp. 337-81.

[38] Wedgwood, I, 474; Paston Letters, V, 109-11; Weever, p. 834.

[39] Samuel Pegge, Curialia: Or an Historical Account Of Some Branches Of The Royal Household, &c. &c., 2 vols. (London, 1791-1806), I, 8-16.

thankys. As well of Kyng Edward hys own souerayn Lord, as of the seid Duke Charles and after the warres doon betwyxt the seid Kynge Lewes, and the seid Duke Charles, Than the seid Thomas Howard returned into England, unto kynge Edward hys souerayn Lord: And he made hym immedyatly Esquyer for hys body."[40] Thomas held office as esquire to the body for several years, probably until sometime in 1477.[41]

Both he and his father went on Edward's military expedition to France in 1475 in which Thomas brought six men at arms and forty archers with him. But Edward IV, and especially Louis XI, had little heart for an unprofitable war, and so the two monarchs met with each other and decided to proclaim a peace based on the newly negotiated Treaty of Picquigny. One of the principal negotiators of the Treaty of Picquigny was John Howard, and with Edward IV and other important nobles, he became a pensioner of the French government.[42] Upon his return to England, Thomas requested the king's permission to withdraw from court and soon settled down to a comfortable life with his family at Ashwelthorpe, Norfolk, serving that shire as a justice of the peace in 1476. He was also sheriff of Suffolk and Norfolk for 1477-78 and was an M.P. for Norfolk in 1477.[43] Fortune continued to smile on

[40] Weever, p. 834. Thomas did serve Charles The Bold, but according to A. R. Myers he did not come home after the second truce but after the first truce between Charles and Louis XI and consequently is mentioned as being esquire to the body in the first service to Edward IV which began in October 1471. Myers, pp. 199, 263.

[41] P.R.O. E 405/60, 61. The last reference to his being an esquire to the body occurs on a patent dated May 22, 1477. C. P. R. 1476-85, p. 37.

[42] P.R.O. E 405/61; Ramsay, II, 411-13. Thomas Howard's epitaph relates that he was with Edward IV at his meeting with Louis XI, and the Milanese ambassador to the Burgundian Court records that at the conference held at Picquigny there was a parley between the French and English kings in which one Master Auart [Howard] took part. Weever, pp. 834-35; C. S. P. Milan, I, 313. Though Thomas was not formally knighted until 1478, he is listed on MS. 2 M. 16 College of Arms as a banneret and his distinctive emblem shown is a salet, a new type of martial headgear just then becoming popular. Francis Pierrepont Barnard (ed.), *Edward IV's French Expedition of 1475: The Leaders and Their Badges being MS. 2 M. 16 College of Arms* (Oxford, 1925), pp. 78-79.

[43] Hamon Le Strange, *Norfolk Official Lists* (Norwich, 1890), pp. 17, 47. During 1476 he was on a commission to look into a complaint that pirates had carried off merchandise from the ship, *la Marie* of Lete, Scotland, and with another person he was granted a piece of woodland called Holbroke Park, Suffolk. Before the year was out he was appointed steward of the lands of the deceased William Lord Morley during the minority of Morley's son, Henry. As sheriff of Norfolk and Suffolk he did such various things as following up the complaint of the despoiling

his father who received many of the de Vere properties in Suffolk and Essex by reason of the attainder of John de Vere, thirteenth earl of Oxford.[44]

Thomas had married on April 30, 1472. His wife was Elizabeth Tylney, the widow of Humphrey Bourchier who had been killed at Barnet, fighting for the Yorkist cause. Elizabeth was wealthy, having manors in Norfolk and Suffolk and other lands in Lincoln, York, Stafford and Cambridge. From the time of his marriage until his wife's death, Thomas made his home at Ashwelthorpe in Norfolk, one of his wife's manors.[45] His marriage to Bourchier's widow was another occasion of disappointment and dissatisfaction to the Pastons, for John Paston, the younger brother of Sir John Paston, had hopes himself of marrying this rich widow. On September 15, 1471 Sir John wrote his brother: "I praye yow sende me worde hoghe ye doo with my Lady Elysabeth Boghscher; ye have a lytell chaffyd it, but I can not tell howe; sende me worde whether ye be in better hope or werse."[46] He had more than a little chafed it and his hopes were worse rather than better. His brother concluded this unhappy episode in the Paston family annals by writing him once again on April 30, 1472 that this day "... my Ladye and yours, Dame Elizbeth Bowgh-cher, is weddyd to the Lorde Howards soon and heyr".[47] Since there had been talk in 1454 of arranging a marriage between Margery Paston and Thomas Howard,[48] the Howard-Tylney alliance was doubly galling to the Pastons. Obviously the strong position which the Howards held at court had helped Thomas in his suit for Dame Bourchier's hand.

Thomas Howard did not have long to wait for the birth of those sons who eventually became Henry VIII's councillors. His son and heir, Thomas, was born in 1473, Edward in 1477, and Edmund about

---

of *la Marie* and summoning the Bishop of Norwich to Chancery in the case of the contumacious Christina Baker. In 1478 he was listed on two commissions of inquiry, one of which was into the lands of the attainted George, duke of Clarence, who had finally paid with his head for his disloyalty to his brother. *C. P. R. 1467-77*, pp. 564, 605, 623. *C. P. R. 1476-85*, pp. 5, 37, 49, 108-11. *C. C. R. 1476-85*, 610.

[44] *C. P. R. 1467-77*, pp. 538, 545-47.

[45] *Paston Letters*, V, 137; *C. I. P. M. H VII*, II, 18, 19; *Memorials*, p. 9; Nicholas Harris Nicolas, *Testamenta Vetusta ...*, 2 vols. (London, 1826), II, 482-83. Hereafter cited as *Test. Vet.*

[46] *Paston Letters*, V, 111.

[47] *Ibid.*, p. 137.

[48] *Paston Letters*, II, 331.

1479. These three children were followed by Muriel and Elizabeth and several other children who died in infancy.[49] When Thomas's father visited Ashwelthorpe in July 1482, he was quite pleased with his grandchildren and he gave the nursery ten shillings.[50]

---

[49] See Table II on page 24.
[50] Collier, p. 222. See Table III on page 26.

II

RISE AND FALL

The Howards's benefactor, Edward IV, was dead, having died on April 9, 1483. During his lifetime Edward Plantagenet knighted and ennobled the elder Howard, raised him to positions of trust as treasurer of the household and member of the king's council and conferred on him the de Vere and other properties. The king nurtured Howard's son Thomas in his royal household: first, as his henchman, then as one of his esquires to the body. The royal influence helped the younger Howard to establish himself as an important figure in Norfolk politics. For over twenty years the Howards basked in the warmth of Edward's favor, and now the lusty, bluff, good-natured king was dead.

He was not a great king, but he did have ability and had he lived longer, there is the distinct possibility that he would have firmly pointed England in the direction of absolute monarchy. Though the pursuit of sensual pleasures was his chief occupation and he lacked the industry of Henry VII, he knew the value of money. By the deal he made at Picquigny in 1475 with Louis XI, he was annually supplied with enough money so that he could dispense with the calling of parliament. Nor was he unfamiliar with the habit of requiring benevolences from his wealthier subjects. He was the first English king in a century who died leaving a fortune. His joviality and masculinity won him the hearts of the London populace, but he did not often turn his popularity to good use. He let his pleasures obscure his duties and he allowed the cause of personal favorites and his wife to sway his judgment. Both James Gairdner and Bishop Stubbs drew unflattering portraits of Edward as a king; neither historian saw him as a great king, but Gairdner's judgment was more temperate than Stubbs's. Gairdner acknowledged Edward's affability, but concluded that Edward was "... a good soldier but a bad general, a jovial companion but a poor statesman".[1] Bishop Stubbs found no conspicuous merits in Edward despite his courage, education, and eloquence, and wrote him off: "But that is all: he was as a man vicious far beyond any king that England had seen since the days of John; and more cruel and bloodthirsty than any king she had ever known: he had too a conspicuous a talent for extortion."[2]

If the morality of Edward's methods in procuring funds were not in question, one might come to a conclusion far different from that of Bishop Stubbs. The prime necessity of the state in Edward's reign was to be solvent; thus, if one measures success by the state of the kingdom's finance, then Edward IV was the most successful monarch since Henry I. After 1471 he brought a measure of stability to the English throne unknown during the past generation. His reign saw a prosperous peace made with France and the extension of the northern borders by his brother Richard, duke of Gloucester. The portrait of Edward as an amiable, but aimless sovereign is not totally satisfactory.

John Howard performed his last service to his departed sovereign on April 16, 1483. As king's bannerer he carried Edward's banner, riding immediately in front of the corpse in the funeral procession. He rode ". . . upon a courser traped with blacke velvet with dyvers scochons of the kinges armes, with his morning hode upon his hede".[3] Once the final obsequies were made for the dead king, thought could be given to the new king — he was Edward V, the twelve year old son of Edward IV. At the time of his father's death he was at Ludlow Castle, Shropshire, keeping his own household and his own council, chief of whom was his uncle Anthony Woodwille, Earl Rivers, the brother of Queen Elizabeth.

Since Edward IV's death had taken most of the nobility by surprise, few were in London. The absence of the Duke of Gloucester, Henry Stafford, duke of Buckingham, and Lord Rivers, added to the usual confusion which accompanies the unexpected death of a king.[4] Since Edward had not yet reached his majority, there was the prospect of a long regency. And in any regency there were many problems which made the routine of government more complex. Instead of the king exercising direct control over the selection of the chief officers of

[1] James Gairdner, *The Houses Of Lancaster And York With The Conquest And Loss Of France* (New York, 1875), p. 209.
[2] William Stubbs, *The Constitutional History Of England In Its Origin And Development*, 5th ed., 3 vols. (London, 1896), III, 226.
[3] *L. P. R III & H VII*, I, 7.
[4] Ramsay, II, 476; *L. P. R III & H VII*, "Preface", I, xvi.

state, influencing the country's foreign policy by his wishes, and determining the standard of justice, there was in his place either a group of councillors constituting the regency or a sole regent acting for the king. Who would decide whether this man or men were acting in accordance with the ancient custom of the realm and in the interest of the child-king? And in times of a regency men were far more aware of the powers exercised in the name of the crown and much more concerned that they should not lose their accustomed privileges.

Moreover, there was the very practical problem of who should be regent. Usually, the late king's council appointed some royal relative as regent or protector. Ideally, the council should select someone who was also well-qualified for the position, but this was not always possible. Consideration had to be given to rank, and sometimes intelligence was no respector of persons. Possibly, as in the case of Edward V, there might be several choices for a protector. Edward V's mother or his uncle Anthony Woodwille, Lord Rivers, or his uncle on his father's side, Richard, duke of Gloucester, could conceivably have been chosen. However, the animosity engendered by the Woodvilles made it unlikely that a Woodville would be chosen. The members of the king's council had little love for the queen who saw her father installed as lord treasurer and married her numerous sisters and brothers to the wealthiest heirs and heiresses in the land. Nor did they feel highly attracted to Rivers whom Queen Elizabeth had wished to marry Mary of Burgundy, Charles the Bold's daughter and heiress. In the eyes of most councillors, the Woodvilles were a presumptuous lot and the less power they had, the better. There was little question that their choice for protector would fall on Richard, duke of Gloucester.

They looked to the good duke to bring order out of disorder. When Edward IV died, the council was literally helpless constitutionally, since the king was the fountain from which flowed all authority and all justice. Whatever the council did, they did in the name of the king. Thus, they wished to settle things as quickly as possible and to clothe their acts with legality. Theoretically, they needed the assent of the king for all actions which they proposed, but this was impossible during a minority. Therefore, it was necessary to bypass the normal channel of authority, and to set up an authority in place of and representative of the minor king's authority. But the council could do little but intrigue until its most important member, Richard, duke of Gloucester, came from his northern residence at Middleham to

London. Even routine matters were not handled by the council until April 21 [5] — the government of England stood paralyzed for nearly a fortnight.

One very pressing problem confronted Richard: the necessity of securing the king's person, for each king in his own person represents the supreme authority of the land. The constitution could not function without him. Since the king's word was law, those in possession of the king's person could control the kingdom through him. Of course, they must have the necessary force to back up their claim, but the king's presence could put law and right on their side. Thus, it was essential for Richard to take his nephew into his care and forestall any attempt on the part of Rivers to rule in the name of Edward V. Steps were immediately taken to prevent Rivers from getting control of the government. At the instigation of William, Lord Hastings, Edward IV's former chamberlain and an enemy of the Woodvilles, and the powerful Henry Stafford, duke of Buckingham, the council forbade Edward V, still in Rivers's care, from bringing more than two thousand men with him to London.

While the council prepared for the coming of Edward V and made plans for his coronation, his uncle Gloucester was making his way to London. Gloucester was met at Northampton by the Duke of Buckingham and Rivers, who had momentarily turned aside from his task of conducting the boy-king, Edward V, to London. Rivers was accompanied by his nephew, Sir Richard Grey, Queen Elizabeth's second son by her first marriage. After being welcomed and royally entertained by Gloucester, Grey and Rivers were summarily seized and sent northward under guard. They had scarcely two months to live, for both were executed in the latter part of June: so much for the chief Woodville threat. Gloucester escorted Edward V the remainder of the way to London, and they arrived in that city on May 4. Nine days later the duke assumed the dignity of Lord Protector of the English realm and on July 6 he was crowned king.[6]

If one reflects on the nature of English monarchy, and particularly on the succession question in the fifteenth century, Richard's determination to be king does not seem as strange or unnatural as it first

[5] Not until April 21, 1483 was government resumed in Edward V's name with the reappointment of the Judges of King's Bench and Common Pleas. On April 27, commissioners for collecting the Alien Tax, among whom were Thomas and John Howard, were appointed for the various counties. Ramsay, II, 477; *C. P. R. 1476-85*, pp. 353-54.

[6] Ramsay, II, 478-96.

appears. He was not the first king who was accused of doing away with a nephew for the crown. This charge was also laid at the feet of King John. By a process of eliminating those closest to the throne, the claims of others less near are advanced. It was a process of simple subtraction based on blood and treason. The floodgates to lawlessness were opened by Bolingbroke when he usurped the crown of that tragic king, Richard II. If the king, the source of all law is deposed, what happens to the idea of law? What justification can be advanced for seizing the throne that cannot as well be advanced against the usurper? Does the idea of the sanctity of the king's person disappear? Obviously, Henry IV's seizure of the crown was a dangerous precedent which later returned to plague his house. The seeds of the Wars of the Roses were sown in 1399, and men could even then contemplate the unhappy consequences of this act which led to an English blood bath. The fifteenth century can be aptly summed up in Shakespeare's words "... time is broke and no proportion kept!".[7]

Because the time was broke and men did not know how to preserve the natural order in government or in their personal lives, the way was open for all manner of unnatural actions. Paradoxically, the very men who most seriously threatened the existing political order: the rival contenders for the crown, such as Henry of Bolingbroke, wholeheartedly accepted the sentiment expressed by Shakespeare's Richard II:

> Not all the water in the rough rude sea
> Can wash the balm off an annoited king;
> The breath of worldly men cannot depose
> The deputy elected by the Lord.[8]

If one counts Richard II, no less than four English kings in the fifteenth century lost their lives either in pursuit of the crown or because they stood in someone's way.

The comparative ease with which Richard III became king raises the interesting question of why the important nobles acceded to his wishes. Fear of the Woodville influence, lack of knowledge of Richard's true designs, confidence in his abilities as an administrator, and hope of future rewards played varying parts in the council

---

[7] William Allan Neilson and Charles Jarvis Hill (eds.), *The Complete Plays and Poems of William Shakespeare* (New York, 1942), p. 629. Hereafter cited as Shakespeare.

[8] *Ibid.*, p. 615.

members' determination to support the usurper. The role played by the Howards in Richard's seizure of power is an important one and sheds light on one of the most famous of all English mysteries: the murder of the little princes in the tower.

The case against the Howards rests on a strong motive and a series of interesting coincidences. John Howard had the strongest of all possible motives for murdering the second little prince, Richard, duke of York and duke of Norfolk. By the parliamentary act of January 16, 1478 it was decreed that this prince, Edward IV's second son, should receive all the Mowbray lands should his wife Anne, the daughter of the deceased John Mowbray, duke of Norfolk, die without heirs. The purpose of this act was to provide for Edward IV's second son without charge to the king. If the little heiress were to die without heirs, the act made her husband, the prince, her heir instead of the co-heirs, John Howard and William Berkeley. In the parliamentary act each of the co-heirs was, however, allowed to assert their right to certain manors, and Thomas Howard was knighted at the marriage of Richard, duke of York, and Anne Mowbray.[9] As long as the little heiress lived, the Howards had little interest in her properties since her heirs of the body and not the Howards would inherit her estates. When she died in 1481[10] at the age of eight, the situation was radically altered and meant that only the little prince stood in the way of John Howard's inheriting his share of the Mowbray properties. But as long as Edward IV lived, John Howard had little hope of getting his hands on these rich lands.

Both Thomas Howard and his father John were intimates of Richard III. Thomas became the steward of Richard's household,[11] and thus was privy to the king's most secret thoughts. Succeeding generations of historians have reviled Thomas for showing "discreditable zeal"[12] in behalf of the Protector and for being "... a strenuous assertor of the Usurper's cause...".[13] And Richard III also held John Howard in high regard, for the two men knew each other from the days of Edward IV and had corresponded and campaigned together. On one occasion Richard's players and actors entertained the Howard

---

[9]   Weever, p. 834; G. E. C., IX, 781; Rot. Parl., VI, 167-70.
[10] G. E. C., IX, 610.
[11] Myers, p. 287.
[12] Dallaway, II, pt. 2, 191.
[13] Owen Manning and William Bray, "Introduction", The History And Antiquities Of The County Of Surrey ..., 3 vols. (London, 1804-14), I, xxv.

household in 1482.[14] And John Howard was constable of the Tower when Richard III succeeded to the throne.

The Howards had the opportunity to do away with the princes and their motivation was personal gain and the desire to please Richard. As constable of the Tower, John Howard supervised preparations for receiving the little princes. Edward V arrived on May 19, but his brother did not join him until June 16. Significantly, June 17 is the last day for which documents can be found with Edward V's signature.[15] The time of the little princes's death must have occurred soon after this date, probably sometime before John Howard's creation as Duke of Norfolk on June 28. John Howard had taken up residence in London on June 5 and so had easy access to the Tower. He had also procured two sacks of lime soon after Edward V was installed in the Tower.[16] Was Howard waiting for the Duke of York to join his brother for the opportunity to use it? Only the death of the Duke of York was essential to Howard, but perhaps he was willing to do away with Edward V for a consideration. The death of both princes was necessary for Richard III's purposes.

The part John Howard played in the Protector's usurpation of the throne was both a conspicuous and significant one. Next to Lord Hastings and the Duke of Buckingham, he was the most important councillor in the inner ring that plotted the Woodville destruction and the Gloucester protectorate. That Howard was friendly with the Protector cannot be disputed; it was a friendship that blossomed from an acquaintanceship struck up in the 1460's to an intimacy which in the 1480's embraced common intellectual, business, and military pursuits. As former comrade-in-arms they could talk plainly to one another. Each had something to give in their new political association: Howard, his trusty arm and the confidence and esteem in which others held him; and Richard, honors, title, and wealth. C. Oman, the author of *The History of England From The Accession of Richard II To The Death of Richard III (1377-1485)*, hints darkly that Howard was indeed "bought" by Richard's intimations that the stewardship

[14] Paul Murray Kendall, *Richard The Third* (London, 1955), pp. 195-96. Hereafter cited as Kendall. See also Turner, pp. 580-81. John Howard sold the manor of Wivenhoe, Essex in 1480 to Richard. *C. C. R. 1476-85*, p. 735.

[15] Ramsay, II, 483-86; Collier, "Introduction", p. xiii; V. B. Lamb, *The Betrayal Of Richard III* (London, 1959), p. 69. Hereafter cited as Lamb. Robert Brackenbury, Richard III's constable, did not take office until July 17, 1483 and, thus, probably had nothing to do with the death of the little princes. See *C. P. R. 1476-85*, pp. 137, 364, 418.

[16] Collier, p. 394.

of the Duchy of Lancaster, granted to Howard on May 14, was only the beginning of future emoluments.[17]

John Howard proved to be a useful accomplice. Ironically, the common people thought that he would be true to this trust to Edward V, for to them he appeared to be a dependable, honest, and honorable royal servant. As long as he participated in the deliberations of the council and watched over the princes, they felt that no harm could come to them. George Cely, writing to George Weston in June, expressed fear for the life of young Edward V if either the Earl of Northumberland or Lord Howard were slain.[18] Of course, Richard, Edward's brother and also Duke of York, was just as important as the little king, since he was the heir apparent to the throne. Should Edward die, Richard would take his place; thus, Gloucester's plan to usurp the throne must take into account both princes. It was imperative to secure the person of Richard, who was held in protective custody by his mother. Here John Howard showed his value to the Protector's cause, for he prevailed upon the queen mother to give up her son.[19] Once both princes were in his power, Gloucester could then address himself to the problem of purging any council members not willing to permit him to become king. No one knows for certain when Richard came to the conclusion that Hastings had to be eliminated. Hastings was a danger to Richard's ambition for the crown, since the former seemed to prefer a regency in which he and Buckingham might run the kingdom with as little help from the Protector as possible. He probably wished a return to the days of Henry VI's minority when a strong council wielded the only power in the realm. Hastings was not the only one who bore watching: Bishops Rotherham and Morton, and even Lord Stanley, seemed a bit shaky in their allegiance. Two council meetings were scheduled for Friday, June 13 — one was a meeting held at Westminster of those loyal to Richard, and the other held at the Tower was really a trap designed to catch Hastings.[20]

To make sure that Hastings came to the appointed Tower meeting, Thomas Howard was sent to fetch him. More's *Richard III*, from

---

[17]   C. Oman, *The History Of England From The Accession Of Richard II. To The Death Of Richard III (1377-1485)* (London, 1906), p. 476.

[18]   Henry Elliot Malden, ed., *The Cely Papers Selections From The Correspondence And Memoranda Of The Cely Family Merchants of the Staple A. D. 1475-1488* (= *Camden Society, 3rd Ser.,* I) (London, 1900), pp. 132-33.

[19]   *D. N. B.,* X, 43.

[20]   Ramsay, II, 476-86.

which this information came, originally did not name Howard but merely said: "The same morning ere he [Hastings] were vp, came a knight vnto him, as it were of curtesy to accompany hym to the connsaile, but of trouth sent by the protector to hast him thitherward, wyth whom he was of secret confedcracy in that purpose, a meane man at that time, and now of gret auctorite." [21] Hall's *Chronicle* fills in the name of the knight as Thomas Howard and relates Hasting's bad dream of the previous night, and the incident of Hastings's horse stumbling along the way to the Tower. [22] The *Chronicle* uses More's *History* as its principal source of information and also tells this interesting story: "This sir Thomas, while the lord Hastynges stayed awhile commonyng with a priest whom he met in the Towrstrete, brake the lordes tale, saiyng to him merely, what my lord I pray you come on, wherefore talke you so long with that priest, you have no nede of a priest yet, & laughed vpon him, as though he would saye, you shall have nede of one sone: But lytle wyst the other what he ment. . . ." [23]

With Hastings safely in the Tower, Richard confronted him with a charge of treason, ordered his immediate execution, and personally saw it done before noon. Rotherham, Morton, and Stanley were arrested, but did not suffer the same fate as Hastings. The two bishops were imprisoned, while Lord Stanley was set free. [24] With the solid backing of the remainder of his councillors, who were "faythful ether for feare or benefyt", [25] Richard could turn to the problem of legitimizing his claim to the throne. The patent roll of Edward V was closed and the parliament which was to have met on the twenty-fifth was countermanded. Then on the twenty-second, Dr. Ralph Shaw, preaching in the presence of Gloucester and Buckingham, expounded on the illegitimacy of Edward IV's children, and two days later Buckingham publicly suggested that Richard take the throne. Finally, on the twenty-fifth, a petition was presented to Richard urging him to take the crown, and the following day Richard installed himself as king in the chair of state in Westminster Hall with John Howard

[21] William Rastell (ed.), *The workes of Sir Thomas More Knyght, sometyme Lorde Chauncellour of England, wrytten by him in the Englysh tonge* (London, 1557), p. 55.

[22] *Hall's Chronicle . . .*, ed. by Henry Ellis (London, 1809), pp. 360-61.

[23] *Ibid.*, p. 361.

[24] Ramsay, II, 485-86.

[25] Henry Ellis (ed.), *Three Books Of Polydore Vergil's English History Comprising The Reigns Of Henry VI, Edward IV, And Richard III* (= Camden Society, 1st Ser., XXIX) (London, 1844), p. 180.

supporting him on the right hand and the Duke of Suffolk on his left. Two days later the Howards received their rewards. John was made Earl Marshal and Duke of Norfolk, and Thomas became Earl of Surrey. At Richard's coronation John Howard was the high steward and Thomas carried the sword of state.[26]

Until researchers are allowed into Arundel Castle to search for the missing letters that passed between John and Thomas Howard, we will never know for certain the exact nature of their role in the princes's deaths. But such are the circumstances connected with their actions during the crucial months of Richard's usurpation and consolidation of power that they may be strongly suspected of murdering them. In the first place, both Howards were intimates of the king; they had his trust and confidence. If he were to decide to rid himself of his nephews, who better than his steward, the son of his old comrade-in-arms? In the second place, both Howards had the opportunity to despatch the princes; the elder Howard as constable of the Tower could commandeer the keys at will. The younger Howard can be considered suspect also, for he was privy to the designs of both his father and Richard. He could easily have done away with the princes with the connivance of his father and the tacit approval of the Protector. Then, there was a strong motive for the murder aside from pleasing Richard. This was the Howards's desire to get their hands on the Mowbray estates then vested in the person of Richard, duke of York and Norfolk. This motive, so strongly lodged in the breast of the elder Howard, could even explain a murder without Gloucester's approval and a later presentation of it done as a *fait accompli*, for both Howards were suitably rewarded for their services to the new king. The new Duke of Norfolk received more than twenty manors formerly held by the deceased Earl Rivers, and Thomas was awarded an annuity of £1,100 which was to be paid during the life of his father.[27] This large land grant and the enormous annuity were "payoffs" as were the previous elevations to the Dukedom of Norfolk and the Earldom of Surrey.[28] Richard III was probably expressing his gratitude for a job well done.

---

[26]   Ramsay, II, 487-95; *C. P. R. 1476-85*, p. 360; see also James Gairdner, *History of the Life and Reign of Richard III*, new ed. (London, 1898), pp. 102-03.

[27]   *C. P. R. 1476-85*, pp. 359, 365, 479; B. M. Add. Ch. 16559. See also B. M. Harl. 433 fols. 74 (r) and 76 (v).

[28]   It was not necessary for Richard III to make the elder Howard a duke and the younger an earl or to give them, along with William Berkeley, the other co-heir who was made Earl of Nottingham, any part of the estates or titles conferred

What is the evidence as to the role played by the Howards in the murder? The account upon which most subsequent reports have been based is More's *Richard III* written about the year 1513 when More was sheriff in the city of London and as such was familiar with the king's treasury and its affairs. A. F. Pollard in "The Making of Sir Thomas More's Richard III" asks the intriguing question, who was More's informant concerning the details in the murder of the princes? After discarding Morton as not being the most probable informer, and noting that certain names and dates were left blank, including the omission of Thomas Howard's names as the "mean" knight sent to get Hastings, Pollard suggests the name of a great many people who were connected with Howard in his capacity as lord treasurer. He then broaches the idea that More's informant must have been Thomas Howard, then earl of Surrey, since who else could have told More the incident of Hastings's horse stumbling and what Hastings said on the fateful day of June thirteenth. The reference to a "mean man" is interpreted as equivalent to mesne, meaning a man of moderate status which Howard certainly was at that time.[29] V. B. Lamb disagrees with Pollard, thinking that Catesby[30] was the man sent for Hastings, but her evidence is vitiated by the fact she has not

---

on Edward IV's second son. He could have kept the property. G. E. C. states that these creations "... either ignored that of Edward IV or tacitly acknowledged that his nephew was dead". G. E. C., IX, 611. There is the strong possibility that the princes were dead and the Howard elevations were for services rendered. The seniority of the co-heirs to the Mowbray estates is not known for certain: the funeral epitaph claims the seniority for the Howards while this claim to priority is also upheld equally as well by the Berkeley claimant. Weever, p. 835. John Smyth, *The Berkeley Manuscripts* ..., ed. by Sir John MacClean, 3 vols. (Gloucester, 1883-85), II, 126. Since Berkeley got the Nottingham title which was lodged in the Mowbray family in 1377 and 1383 and thus, anterior to the Mowbray creation as dukes of Norfolk (1397) there is a strong probability that the older title was given to the co-heir in the right of his prior descent. The fact that the lands he got in the division between the co-heirs embodied the old Mowbray estates lends credence to the idea that his mother was the older sister. G. E. C., IX, 780-81; *Rot. Parl.*, VI, 206. Berkeley's feelings of dissatisfaction at having "... too much land, and too little honor ..." may have been inspired by the thought that he and not the elder Howard should have been made duke and earl marshal. Smyth, II, 126.

[29] A. F. Pollard, "The Making Of Sir Thomas More's Richard III", in *Historical Essays In Honour Of James Tait*, ed. by J. G. Edwards, V. H. Galbraith, and E. F. Jacob (Manchester, 1933), pp. 224-28. Even if More were not the author, it would be dangerous for one writing in Henry VIII's reign to speak of the Howard's connection to Richard III since the Howards were a very powerful family.

[30] Lamb, p. 78.

considered Pollard's article nor the possibility of Howard's involvement in the murder.

To reinforce his point, Pollard notes that John Howard is not mentioned in the entire text, that Thomas is not mentioned by name, and that Thomas's son, Thomas II, is only introduced on the first page as the husband of Edward IV's daughter, Anne. He concludes: "So far as More's *Richard III* is concerned, the Howards might not have existed." [31] And even Richard III's coronation was only given two lines in the Latin edition. Why this conspiracy of silence? Obviously the Howards were returning to favor in 1513 and were much too powerful to be mentioned. Pollard strongly intimates that the reason for numerous errors of fact in More's *Richard III* springs from the author's desire to write drama and thus, he sacrificed history for dramatic effect. Some of the facts misused were the date of Edward IV's birth, an error about the Queen giving up the prince before, instead of after, June thirteenth, and Sir James Tyrrel's knighthood as coming after the bloody deed, when in fact he had been knighted by Edward IV at Tewkesbury in 1471. [32]

Is one satisfied, though, with the answer that the facts are consistently abused to tell a good story? Can one not conjecture that since More's *Richard III* is largely the outcome of oral testimony, that the person giving this testimony deliberately misled his listener and thus, confused generations of historians? Why should the precise date of the coming of the second prince to the Tower be concealed, if not to protect the Howards, who otherwise might be more specifically linked to the crime? And the fantastic tale of the murder involving Tyrrel, Brackenbury, Dighton, and Forest in which there are errors of fact: could it not have been invented to throw people off the Howard scent and lead them not to suspect that the princes were murdered earlier than commonly supposed, probably before the Howard elevation to the Dukedom of Norfolk?

The conspiracy of silence enjoined by More's narration of the Howard part in those dark days of June and July 1483 lends credence to the case against the Howards. Even Thomas's funeral epitaph, usually a fountain of information on his activities, has little to say of his services to Richard III. After stating, that since the Mowbray heiress died without issue, that he and his father secured their rightful titles as Surrey and Norfolk, it continues that "... they both serued

[31] Pollard, *loc. cit.*, p. 229.
[32] *Ibid.*, pp. 229-33.

the seid kinge Rychard truly as his Subgettis durynge his lyff, lyeng at home in their owne Countries and kepyng honorable howsses".[33] The idea conveyed is that the Howards performed no more duties for Richard III than they would have for any other king; in fact, less since they stayed at home. It leaves out all mention of the reliance which Richard placed on them — a reliance, it might be added, which later placed Thomas in jeopardy of his life, for so intimately was he connected with Richard that he was listed third on the November 1485 act of attainder against Richard's supporters.[34]

During Richard's reign the Howards were frequently with him. As steward of the household, Thomas, now earl of Surrey, would have been in constant attendance on his sovereign. That autumn both Howards participated in the military operations against Buckingham, who provoked the local uprising in Exeter to proclaim as king, Henry Tudor, earl of Richmond and the Lancastrian claimant to the throne. The revolt was unsuccessful and Buckingham was executed for his part in it.[35] Surrey was sent with seven others to array Sussex and Kentishmen for the purpose of besieging Bodiam Castle, which was still held by the rebels. During the next year, the Howards went to Parliament and were on the usual commissions of the peace, array, and gaol delivery.[36] In addition to other rewards, the Howards were given the wardship of the youthful Henry, earl of Essex; Surrey was made steward of the Duchy of Lancaster for all Norfolk lands, and his father received the castle and lordship of Farley and the late Duke of Buckingham's office of master of game in Norfolk.[37] The new Duke of Norfolk was employed in a great deal of government business: he was the admiral of England, and was given power to array the king's subjects in the thirteen eastern shires. He was a commissioner to treat with the Scots, and was one of the first of Richard's subjects sent for on the reception of the news that Henry Tudor had landed on English soil.[38]

---

[33] Weever, p. 835.
[34] *Rot. Parl.*, VI, 276.
[35] *Paston Letters*, VI, 73; Ramsay, II, 506-07.
[36] *C. P. R. 1476-85*, pp. 370, 397, 400, 465, 488-90, 519, 553, 566-80. They also participated in the trial of the traitor William Colingbourne. Kendall, pp. 300-01.
[37] *C. P. R. 1476-85*, p. 501; B. M. Harl. 433 fols. 24 (v), 29 (v), 162 (r). I am indebted to Mrs. V. B. Lamb for permitting me to use her name index to Harl. 433. For other pertinent grants see B. M. Harl. 433 fols. 24 (v), 33 (r), 52 (r), 96 (v), 97 (v), 161 (v), 162 (r), 186 (r), and *C. P. R. 1476-85*, pp. 411, 497, 510.
[38] *C. P. R. 1476-85*, pp. 362-63; Gairdner, *Richard III*, p. 226.

The Howards did not hesitate, but hastened to join Richard at Leicester. Having placed their trust in the king and having identified their fortunes with his from the first, Thomas and John Howard determined to pour all their energies into his defence. The night preceding Bosworth someone is supposed to have tacked up this inscription on Norfolk's tent:

> Jack of Norfolk, be not too bold,
> For Dickon [Richard III], thy Master is bought and sold.[39]

If this was so, neither the duke nor his son heeded the warning, but bravely marshalled their forces for the coming engagement and then plunged into the thick of the battle. Norfolk fell while commanding the van, and Thomas, grievously wounded, was surrounded and taken prisoner to be put in the Tower of London.[40] John Beaumont's famous poem "Bosworth Field" graphically describes the last moments of John Howard, who while fighting with John de Vere, the earl of Oxford, was struck down by an arrow. Meanwhile, Thomas decided he could continue fighting no longer and begged Sir Gilbert Talbot to despatch him lest someone of non-gentle blood kill him. Talbot refused, and Surrey was taken prisoner.[41] Then came Surrey's famous rejoinder to Talbot's question as to why the earl had fought for that tyrant Richard:

> Set England's royall wreath vpon a stake,
> There will I fight, and not the place forsake. . . .[42]

While the Howards were overcome fighting in the van, Richard threw himself into the thick of the fight and died manfully defending his right to wear the crown. As the story goes, one of Henry's supporters plucked the crown from a bramble bush and placed it upon the victor's brow: he was now Henry VII, king by virtue of his conquest and soon to be recognized as *de jure* king by parliament. With

---

[39] *Ibid.*, 243.

[40] Gairdner, *Lancaster And York*, p. 234; Weever, p. 835.

[41] Alexander B. Grosart (ed.), *The Poems Of Sir John Beaumont, Bart. For The First Time Collected And Edited With Memorial-Introduction and Notes* (Beachburn, Lancashire, 1869), pp. 48-51.

[42] *Ibid.*, p. 51. William Camden also repeats the story, but in Camden's narration it is Henry VII, not Talbot, who asks Surrey the question and he replied: "He was my crowned King, and if the Parlamentary authority of England sette the crowne vppon a stocke, I will fight for that stocke. And as I fought then for him, I will fight for you, when you are established by the said authoritie." William Camden, *Remains . . .* (London, 1605), p. 217.

Henry VII's accession and the defeat of Richard,[43] Thomas Howard's fortunes sank to their lowest ebb. He had served two Yorkist kings with all his power, and that service had not gone unnoticed by either Edward or Richard. For the most part, they had deserved his loyalty and their treatment of him suggests a high regard for his abilities and personal qualities. With the rise of Richard, Thomas came into his own as a prominent court figure. He was one of those useful people, able to do a multitude of tasks and willing to do whatever the king willed. His position as steward of the royal household was an admirable post for a man of his talents, but it also marked him for special treatment by the new king.

From the vaunted pre-eminence of being an intimate of kings, Surrey was cast into the Tower. He was attainted by the parliament of November 7, 1485 and, thus, lost his title and his lands. By the legal fiction that Henry VII had become king the day before Bosworth, Richard's supporters were technically guilty of treason for having fought against Henry and so were subject to an act of attainder. Thomas was the third named person in the act of attainder, coming after King Richard and his father, the Duke of Norfolk. Not only did the earl suffer from the attainder, but his wife and children suffered as well.[44] There was one clause that provided some solace to the troubles of the attainted's family. This was that the wife might "... freely enjoy, have and possede, after the dethe of her Husband, all her owne Inheretaunce, to her and to her heyres, other than ben atteinted or unhabled by thys acte...".[45] But Surrey was alive and, thus, some benefactor appointed by the king probably looked after his wife and family who lived at Ashwelthorpe during his imprisonment.[46] Before taking her children to Ashwelthorpe, Surrey's wife had cause to complain of her treatment and wrote from the Isle of Shepey to John Paston on October 3, 1485:

Cosyn, I shewyd you myn mynde that I wolde have myn shildren to Thorpe, wher in, God yelde you, it pleasyd you to sey that I shulde have hors of you to help conveye them thyder; but now I undirstonde myn Lord Fitz Walter [John Ratcliff] hath dischargyd myn lordys servauntes thens, affermyng up on them that they shulde have had unfittyng langage of the Kynges Grace. Cosyn, I trust that ye and all the jentilmen of the shire, which have had knowleche of myn lordes servauntes, kan sey that her to for they have not

---

[43]   Ramsay, II, 449-50; Kendall, p. 367.
[44]   *Rot. Parl.*, VI, 267-76.
[45]   *Ibid.*, 276.
[46]   *Memorials*, Appendix VI.

ben of that disposicion to be lavas of theyr tungys, whan they had moore cause of booldness than they have nowe. I wolde not have thowght my Lord Fitzwalter wolde have takyn so ferforth displeasure for the keepyng of x. or xij. men at Thorpe; I woot weell ther exceded not iij. mees [party of four at dinner] meet, good and bad. I truste, all thow I weer a soel woman, to mayntene so many at the leeste, what so evyr I dyde moore.

I trustyd to have fowndyn myn Lord Fitzwalter better lord to me, seyng when I was wyth myn Lord of Oxenforth, up on myn desyre and request at that tyme made un to hym, he promysed me to be good lord to myn lord and me, wher of I praye you to put hym in remembrauns, trustyng yit be the meene of you to fynde hym better lord to me her aftyr.

I have fownde myn Lord of Oxenforthe singuler very good and kynde lord to myn lord and me, and stedfaste in hys promys, wher by he hath wonne myn lordys service as longe as he leevyth, and me to be hys trewe beedwoman terme of my lyve; for hym I drede mooste, and yit as hyther to I fynde hym beste. I pray you good cosyn, the rather by your meane, that I may have the continuans of hys good lordship, and to myn poore power I truste to deserve it.[47]

Shortly after Surrey was put in the Tower there was a rumor to the effect that he would soon be released. Giovanni De Gigles, Collector of Peter's Pence in England, wrote on December 6, 1485 to the pope that Henry Percy, earl of Northumberland had been set free and that soon Surrey was to be freed.[48] There was little truth in this rumor. Three days after De Gigles's letter was written, Sir James Radcliff, lieutenant of the Tower, submitted a list of costs for boarding various people[49] and among the items was this one: "Item, for the bourding of the erle of Surrey by the space of iiij. wokes every woke at xl. s – viii. li. Item, for the bourding of iij. men of the said erle by the space of iiij. wokes, xxx s."[50] Forty shillings a week was a considerable sum to expend on the maintenance of one man. In fact, Surrey was getting more in one week than was spent in four weeks for his three retainers. Even gentlemen such as David Lloyd and John Say had only six shillings and eight pence devoted to them per week.[51] The obvious answer to why Surrey was allocated such a large sum for board is that Tower prisoners received board commensurate with rank.

Towards the end of March 1486, Henry VII decided what to do

---

[47] *Paston Letters*, VI, 87-88.
[48] *C. S. P. Ven.*, I, 506; William Campbell (ed.), *Materials For A History Of The Reign Of Henry VII*, 2 vols. (London, 1873-77), I, 198-99. Hereafter cited as Campbell.
[49] *Ibid.*, p. 207.
[50] *Ibid.*, p. 208.
[51] *Ibid.*

with the unfortunate earl. Surrey was to be pardoned of all treason and felony, lose his dignity as an earl, and be imprisoned at the king's pleasure in any prison selected by his majesty despite the general pardon.[52] He was a political prisoner who was too dangerous to be set free. While Surrey was in the Tower, the other co-heir to the Mowbray inheritance, William Berkeley, managed to have conferred on him the office of earl marshal, which had formerly been held by John Howard, duke of Norfolk.[53] The lands that Norfolk had amassed were taken by the crown to be used as it saw fit. Offices in many of the Howard manors were given to Henry VII's supporters and money from the issues thereof.[54] The Sussex manors were granted to Thomas West, lord de la Warre, for a rent of fifty pounds a year[55] and the ducal castle of Framlingham plus other manors in Suffolk and Bedford were given to the Earl of Oxford ". . . to hold until the king provides for him in lands or rents in the realm of the same value".[56] Some of these properties were still in de Vere's possession in 1488-89, as a receivers account for this year shows.[57] It is difficult to determine why Henry VII did not grant the lands outright to Oxford. Perhaps the king had an idea that he might someday regrant them to Thomas Howard if ever he set him free.

For three and one-half years, Henry VII kept the former Earl of Surrey in confinement. Except for the item relating to costs for Surrey's board at the Tower and to the fantastic story perpetuated by his epitaph, that the Lieutenant of the Tower offered him his freedom during the rebellion of the Earl of Lincoln in 1487,[58] there is no evidence of what happened to him, where he was kept, or what efforts he made to secure his freedom. While others prospered in serving the new king and in establishing the new authority, he led a passive existence. The king, the sower of the kernels of royal favor, cast none in his direction: he lay unused, vegetating, and yet fallow. Important events happened without his knowledge or participation. Henry VII had his right to the crown affirmed by parliament, married Elizabeth Plantagenet, Edwards IV's eldest daughter, announced the birth of an

[52] *Ibid.*, p. 392; *C. P. R. 1485-94*, p. 86.
[53] *C. P. R. 1485-94*, p. 74.
[54] *Ibid.*, p. 196; Campbell, I, 309, 319; II, 40, 53, 138, 199, 219, 319.
[55] *C. P. R. 1485-94*, p. 128.
[56] *Ibid.*, p. 121.
[57] Essex Record Office D/Dpr/139. I am indebted to Miss Susan Flower for a transcript of this document.
[58] *L. P. R III & H VII*, "Preface", II, liv; Weever, p. 835.

heir, Prince Arthur, and put down the rebellion of the pretender, Lambert Simnel. While Henry VII choked off the weeds of rebellion and husbanded the resources of his kingdom by encouraging trade and admonishing thrift, the earl, stripped of his great rank and denied access to the king's person, remained a prisoner.

III

LIEUTENANT OF THE NORTH *

Early in 1489, Henry VII gave Surrey his liberty. Why did the king, usually regarded as a shrewd, calculating, but unmerciful sovereign, choose to release the unfortunate earl and, as Francis Bacon relates, immediately grant him his "special favour".[1] At first, Henry's motive seems difficult to discern, but the parliamentary act of 1489 which reversed Surrey's attainder, sheds light on the quality of Henry's mercy. By this act, Thomas Howard was permitted to assume the dignity of Earl of Surrey, but not that of Duke of Norfolk, though his father's attainder had also been reversed. Moreover, not only was Surrey excluded from the dukedom, which he did not receive until 1514 as a new creation at the hands of Henry VIII, but he was specifically excluded from inheriting the Howard patrimony, which included the Howard portion of the Mowbray estates. He was, however, allowed to enjoy those lands which he formerly held in the right of his wife, and provision was made to return his lands which the king had granted to Giles Dawbeney and the Earl of Oxford. Additional parliamentary acts passed in 1490 and 1492 restored his right to all his father's properties, excluding grants of Richard III, and insured that he would inherit the Mowbray properties on the death of the dowager duchess of Norfolk. Accordingly, when Elizabeth Mowbray, the old duchess, died in 1507, Surrey took possession of his lands.[2]

---

* For background material for this chapter I have used the detailed work, R. R. Reid, *The King's Council In The North* (London, 1921), and the excellent pamphlets, F. W. Brooks, *York And The Council Of The North*, St. Anthony's Hall, No. 5 (London, 1954) and F. W. Brooks *The Council Of The North* (= *Historical Association General Series*, G. 25) (London, 1953).

[1] Joseph Devey (ed.), *The Moral And Historical Works Of Lord Bacon, Including His Essays, Apophthegms, Wisdom Of The Ancients, New Atlantis And Life Of Henry The Seventh* (London, 1852), p. 356. Hereafter cited as Bacon, *Henry VII.*

[2] *Rot. Parl.*, VI, 409-11, 426-28, 448-49; *C. P. R. 1494-1509*, p. 543. Bishop Mandell Creighton thinks that Henry VII did not appreciate Surrey's service and

That there was method in Henry's mercy does not detract from its essential mercifulness. It was a great thing for the king to set free one of Richard III's chief officers, especially when one considers the still unsettled state of the kingdom. Henry had withstood two major rebellions, those of Lovel and Simnell, while Surrey was in prison, and at the time of his release another was brewing in the North. The limitations placed on Surrey's inheritance were guarantees that the earl would be so reduced in his means that he would need to accept royal employment to maintain himself in the dignity of an earl. And the hope of future rewards from the hand of his king could be a strong deterrent to rebellion: better to accept largess at the hands of a crowned king, than to risk life and limb for an uncrowned pretender. Henry Tudor's person represented the power and majesty of the English crown — Henry knew it, and he suspected that his servant, Surrey, knew it. The course of events was to show that Henry correctly judged Surrey's character. Others might rebel and do treason to the house of Tudor, but Surrey would serve it faithfully.

Henry's act of clemency was perfectly consistent with his character and assuredly a manifestation of the king's might. In 1486, Henry had not hesitated to free Henry Percy, the earl of Northumberland, an avowed Yorkist. He did this because he needed the earl's help in ruling the troublesome North, where the earl became his chief representative as Lieutenant of the North. His faith in the earl was rewarded by Northumberland's able performance of his official duties

---

showed his displeasure by withholding the earl's confiscated lands until just before he died in 1509. *D. N. B.*, X, 63. Actually, Bishop Creighton is in error; the proximity between the time of Surrey's entry into the Mowbray properties and the time of the king's death may have given credence to the story that Henry withheld the greater portion of Surrey's estates. The only property not given to the earl during Henry's lifetime was his portion of the Fitz-Alan inheritance. The Fitz-Alan inheritance involves land not entailed to males devolving on Elizabeth Fitz-Alan, daughter of Richard, earl of Arundel (d. 1397), and mother of Margaret and Isabel Mowbray. Heirs were to shares of one-fourth were Sir John Wingfield, Thomas Stanley, earl of Derby, Maurice Berkeley, and Surrey. An additional complication was that some land devolved in equal shares to Elizabeth and her sister Jane whose heir was George Neville. This meant a division of such property into a one-half portion for Neville and shares of one-eighth to Elizabeth's heirs. Surrey recovered his share in these properties through a parliamentary act of 1512 while Maurice Berkeley secured his title to the lands in 1504. It may have been that lands recovered by Surrey were encompassed in lands granted by William Berkeley, late earl of Nottingham, to Henry VII, and these lands were specifically excepted from the 1504 act for Maurice Berkeley with the king to enjoy such properties against Berkeley and Howard. Smyth, II, 60; *J. H. L.*, I. vii; *Rot. Parl.*, VI, 530.

— duties which ultimately led to his death. Just as freeing Northumberland demonstrated Henry's confidence in his own ability to handle any situation in which Percy might become involved, the liberation of Surrey showed that the king feared no Yorkist. The king took a certain risk in employing popular Yorkists, but it was a calculated risk where the benefits accrued usually outweighed the chances taken. In addition, the use of his former enemies in Henry's government was an effective form of propaganda for the new Tudor dynasty. The loyalty of these men, especially powerful and popular men like Surrey and Northumberland, set an example for all Englishmen. Indeed, the measure of a kingdom's strength often may be found in the character of her royal servants and in the nature of their loyalty to her sovereign. The authority of the crown attracts, compels, and inspires the loyalty of its servants, but only to such a degree as the person wearing the crown merits such devotion.

Henry VII has been a much maligned man. It is easy to write him off as a niggardly, avaricious, Welsh parvenu. Shakespeare never bothered to write a play about him since he did not have the heroic measurements of a national hero as Henry V, or the fatal defects of character as Richard II or Richard III. Success, especially financial success, did not stagger the Shakesperean imagination as it does that of modern man. Subtle simplicity creates little interest or amusement for the playgoer: the infirmities of the mind, cruel, unnatural, unusual acts, and tragedy, whether caused by defect of the blood or fate, do. Even Polydore Vergil's portrait of Henry is so perfect it is boring. Here, according to Vergil, is a king who is brave, resolute, prudent, scholarly, liberal, and wise. The author embellishes his patron's physical attributes, despite the fact that the king was underweight, had small, beady eyes, thin hair, a sallow complexion and bad teeth.[3] Readers of Bacon's history of Henry VII perpetuate the myth of an unattractive, uninteresting, dull, parsimonious king. They do not focus on Henry's positive achievements; they choose to remember the quotations which confirm their prejudice that he was miserly. For example: "A fame of a war he [Henry VII] liked well, but not an achievement; for the one he thought would make him richer, and the other poorer...."[4] They fail to remember that Bacon considered

[3] *The Anglica Historia Of Polydore Vergil A. D. 1485-1537*, ed. and trans. by Denys Hay (= *Camden Society*, N. S., LXXIV) (London, 1950), p. 145. Hereafter cited as Polydore Vergil.
[4] Bacon, *Henry VII*, p. 340.

Henry to be "... the best lawgiver to this nation, after King Edward the First: for his laws, whoso marks them well, are deep, and not vulgar; not made upon the spur of a particular occasion for the present, but out of providence of the future, to make the estate of his people still more and more happy; after the manner of the legislators in ancient and heroical times." [5]

If Henry is given due regard for his capacity as a lawgiver and his attempts to maintain law and order, he emerges in a more favorable light. The compelling need of the country was for peace based on an established royal authority. Sir John Fortescue, the tutor to Henry VI's only son, writing earlier in the century, recognized the want of governance in the English realm: Henry supplied that need. His justice was a harsh Old Testament justice, but a necessary justice, which he made palatable and effective by efficient administration. Unquestionably, Henry's reputation rests on his administrative talents. The dominant notes in his administration were meticulous attention to detail, the curtailing of expense in domestic management, and shrewd forays into European diplomacy. Henry left his mark, the stamp of his personality, on whatever he did, from the pages of the account books, which he scrupulously initialed, to the working out of diplomatic relations between France and England. Here was an unusual master for Surrey to serve: one who by keeping the thousand and one details of government at his fingertips and by channeling his energy to encompass the governance of his realm in his own person, made it impossible for future historians to tell where his atttudes and concept of government left off and the work and advice of his councillors began.

Immediately upon releasing Surrey, Henry presented him with the important job of restoring order in the unruly northern shires. Violence had occurred when an angry mob of Yorkshiremen met the earl of Northumberland near Thirsk on April 28, 1489 and slew him. The cause of this unhappy riot was northern resistance to the payment of a subsidy granted by the parliament of 1487. The murder of the earl touched off a series of local riots, and the country's unrest was soon made into a revolt of major proportions under the leadership of Sir John Egremont and John à Chambre. Decisive action was called for: the king appointed Surrey, captain of the van of his army, and determined to put down the uprising by military action. He decided

---

[5] *Ibid.*, p. 358.

to go North himself, but before he arrived at the scene of the rebellion, Surrey, who preceded the king northwards, had suppressed it.[6] A commission of oyer and terminer was issued to the earls of Surrey, Oxford, Derby, Shrewsbury, and Thomas Dacre, Guy Fayrefax, and others for the purpose of hearing and settling matters involving the recent offenses committed in York.[7] The rebel leader, John à Chambre, was hanged on a high gallows at York while his associate in rebellion, Sir John Egremont, escaped the country, finding refuge at the court of Margaret of Burgundy. The king himself visited York to see that all was in order, but left after a brief stay, leaving the collection of the tax to his trusted councillors, Richard Tunstall and Thomas Howard, earl of Surrey.[8] Henry gave a special charge to Surrey to be his Lieutenant in the North Parts and for this purpose gave him the office of deputy warden of the marches for the infant Prince Arthur, his first born son.[9] A patent issued to Surrey a year later (May 20, 1490) confirmed his appointment as deputy warden and enlarged upon the nature of his duties. The earl was to have ". . . full power to array the men of Northumberland in the same manner as Henry Percy, knight, sometime warden of the said marches, arrayed the same and to muster them for the defence of the town and castle of Berwick; with power to treat with the subjects of James, king of Scotland touching all infractions of the truce and certify them to the king and council, and to inquire of all persons who have covin with the enemy and punish them."[10] In addition, he held the office of Justice of the Forests North of the Trent[11] and was placed on the commissions of the peace for Northumberland, Cumberland, and the ridings of Yorkshire. He remained a commissioner of the peace for Northumberland until 1502, for Cumberland and Yorkshire until

---

[6] "The Yorkshire Rebellion In 1489", *Gents. Mag.*, N. S. XXXVI, pt. 2 (1851), 459-66; J. D. Mackie, *The Earlier Tudors 1485-1558* (Oxford, 1957), pp. 90-91. Hereafter cited as Mackie.

[7] Charles L. Kingsford (ed.), *Chronicles of London* (Oxford, 1905), p. 194; *C. P. R. 1485-94*, p. 285.

[8] Thomas Allen, *A New And Complete History Of The County Of York*, 6 vols. (London, 1829-31), I, 104.

[9] Campbell, II, 480; P.R.O. C 66/569.

[10] *C. P. R. 1485-94*, p. 314; P.R.O. C 66/570. Although cited in this patent as deputy warden for the east and middle marches, the west march was under his jurisdiction as will be shown below.

[11] Weever, p. 836. This is an office also held by Richard Neville, the famous earl of Warwick; by Richard Plantagenet, before he became Richard III; by Surrey's immediate predecessor Henry Percy, fourth earl of Northumberland; and by Henry Fitzroy, Henry VIII's natural son. Reid, pp. 486-87.

1499.[12] He resided at the king's royal manor of Sheriff Hutton of which he became the constable and steward.

Surrey's tenure as Lieutenant of the North lasted ten years and is of more than passing interest to the historian, for during this time the turbulent North was restored to order and peace negotiated with the Scottish enemy. The term Lieutenant of the North or Lieutenant of the North Parts has often been applied to Surrey, though there seems to be no patent enrolled giving him this title. His own epitaph cites him as Lieutenant-General from the Trent northward,[13] while a predecessor, John de la Pole, the earl of Lincoln, sent north by Richard III is called President of the Council of the North by the noted historian James Gairdner,[14] and a successor to Surrey, Thomas Savage, Archbishop of York, styled himself "... the Kings lieutenant and high commissionar withynne these North parties of his realme...".[15] The variety of descriptive terms applied to the king's chief representative in the North country indicates the complexity of the problem facing the historian who attempts to determine the constitutional powers of the lieutenant. The term lieutenant merely signifies a representative or deputy of the king, and it is undoubtedly in this context that Henry VII referred to the earl as "... our lieutenant and chieff officer ther...",[16] when writing to the York city council. At first glance the term Lieutenant of the North suggests a more complete jurisdiction than does lieutenant-general, which is primarily a military term used in individual commissions to designate a military commander for a specific military operation, as in the case of the appointments of Surrey's son, Thomas, as lieutenant-general of an English force to fight against the Scots in 1523 and a similar commission granted in 1522 to the earl of Shrewsbury.[17] One must note that

---

[12]   C. P. R. 1485-94, pp. 484, 495-96, 506-07; C. P. R. 1494-1509, pp. 634, 652-53, 666-68. Surrey was not listed as a commissioner of the peace for the West Riding of Yorkshire until 1496, though he was a commissioner for the East and North Ridings throughout his tenure as Lieutenant of the North.

[13]   Weever, p. 836.

[14]   L. P. R III & H VII, I, lxviii. George Ridpath, the famous historian of the borders, saw little difference in the terms president or lieutenant, both of which he used to describe Surrey's predecessor, Henry Percy, earl of Northumberland. George Ridpath, The Border History Of England And Scotland, Revised by Philip Ridpath (Berwick, 1848), p. 317.

[15]   Angelo Raine, ed., York Civic Records, Yorks Arch. Soc. Rec. Ser., Vols. XCVIII, CIII, CVI, CVIII, CX, CXII, CXV, CXIX (Wakefield, 1939-53), CVI, 5. Hereafter cited as Raine.

[16]   Raine, CIII, 66.

[17]   L. P., III, 2412; Foedera, XIII, 781-82.

there is specific mention of Surrey in Shrewsbury's commission, that the Earl of Shrewsbury when he "... goes against the Scots he shall have as large entertainment as the Duke of Norfolk, then earl of Surrey, had as King's lieutenant".[18]

That Surrey held no patent as Lieutenant of the North is not proof that he did not hold the office. The Earl of Warwick, the famous Kingmaker, had been appointed Lieutenant of the North by Edward IV by word of mouth,[19] and it is quiet possible, and indeed probable, that Surrey had an oral commission of lieutenancy. Since the earl held an oral commission to be constable and steward of Sheriff Hutton, this seems likely. In the Ministers Accounts for the year 1491-92 there occurs the following entry: "And in fee to Thomas earl of Surrey constable of the castle of Shireffehoton occupying the said office by order of the lord king by word of mouth at 100s per year...."[20] And a similar entry for his post as steward of the royal castle contains the words "... per mandatum domini Regis oretenus...".[21] It would appear then, that Surrey occupied his post as Lieutenant of the North through an oral commission.

The constitutional nature of the earl's duties as Lieutenant of the North can be reconstructed from his actions and the specific commissions issued to him individually and jointly with other councillors. His duties were both civil and military. In view of his place on the commissions of the peace for Northumberland, Cumberland, and the ridings of Yorkshire, and his post of Justice of Forests beyond the Trent, it is logical to assume that his civil jurisdiction was the same as his military jurisdiction: north from the Trent to the Scottish border. There is at least one commission issued to Surrey which commands him to publish a royal proclamation in the counties of Westmorland, Cumberland, York, and Northumberland.[22] Though he was deputy warden-general to both Arthur and Prince Henry, successive warden-generals for the three marches, east, middle, and west, Surrey's contact with affairs of the western march was slight. During the first year of his tenure as Lieutenant of the North, however, he was named as one of the English commissioners to treat with the Scots regarding the right of fishing in the fishgarths of the Eske estuary located on

[18] L. P., III, 2412.
[19] Reid, p. 73.
[20] P.R.O. DL 29/10516. Translated from Latin.
[21] Ibid. Italics mine.
[22] C. P. R. 1485-94, p. 322.

the border of the west march. He was named in a subsequent commission dealing with this matter in 1491.[23] Regardless of the amount of work he performed, he did on occasion receive payment as keeper of the west march.[24] Thus, it is apparent that the extent of Surrey's civil jurisdiction extended from the river Trent to the river Tweed, excluding the palatinate of Durham, which was a separate jurisdiction, but including the three English marches and Yorkshire.

His chief duties in civil matters were: to publish royal proclamations, to suppress riots, and to administer justice in all causes submitted to him. Originally, he had come to Yorkshire to put down a rebellion; he now stayed to keep the peace. His residence, the royal castle of Sheriff Hutton, was about ten miles northeast of the city of York[25] and gave him easy access to this, the most important of the northern cities. Not only was the city the focal point for northern discontent, but it was also the chief place used to assemble English troops prior to the taking of offensive and defensive military action against the Scots. His immediate task was to secure the peace in Yorkshire, an always difficult and persistent problem. Though there is no record that Surrey and his council had a commission of oyer and terminer for use in handling riots, the earl had some sort of royal charge to suppress civil disturbances and misbehaviours. One finds Henry VII writing in March 1491 to the Mayor of York, advising the Mayor that he has written to Surrey ". . . our lieutenaunt and chieff officer in the contrey ther, to call you afor hym if in any wise ye be founden remisse or negligent in reformyng this matier, and he thereupon to yeve you dieu injunction in oure name to see the said mysdeds duely correctid, and if ye fail, then he to certifie us of the same in all goodily hast to thentent that we may provide some othre wayse and menes for the refourmacion and punisshent of the said matier."[26] Henry VII's command is reminiscent of item five in Richard III's instructions of 1484 to the council in the north, that the council have ". . . auctorite and power to ordre and direct alle riottes, forcible entres, distresse takinges, variaunces, debates and other mysbehiavors ayenst our lawes and peas committed and done in the said parties. And if suche be that they in no wise can thoroughly ordre, than to referre it unto us, and

[23] C.D.R. Scot., IV, 1559. Rot. Scot., II, 498.
[24] P.R.O. E405 (2)/78. In one commission of array directed to Surrey he was also cited as keeper of the west march. P.R.O. C 66/576.
[25] George Todd, Castellum Huttonicum: Some Account Of Sheriff-Hutton Castle (York, 1824), p. 3.
[26] Raine, CIII, 66.

thereof certifie us in all goodly hast thereafter."[27] The similarity between the instructions of the two kings for the governance of the North suggests a similar approach to the northern problem.

Without question, Surrey and his council had authority similar to that of a commission of oyer and terminer. Surrey's quick action in extinguishing a small rebellion in the western part of Yorkshire during 1492 and administering justice to the insurrectionists proves this. With the help of the king's subjects, Surrey met the rebels at Ackworth, which is near Pomfret Castle, and completely subdued them. After the battle, the earl put the rebel leaders to death, but showed leniency to their followers whose pardon he secured from the king and by this action won the country's favor.[28] During the battle, Surrey lost a valuable gelding which he was certain had been taken by one of Robert Plumpton's men. In no uncertain terms Surrey required its return; he wrote Plumpton on May 6, 1492:[29] "Cosen, I have some proofe that your servant Robert Beck hath my gelding; one knoweth him well, told it me. I pray you, Cosen, fail not to send me the geldinge with the hand. Your loving cozen, Thomas Surrey."[30]

The Ackworth incident indicates only one of the problems handled by Surrey as he and his council attempted to maintain peace and order in the North. He was intimately involved in the administration of justice in the northern counties, particularly in Yorkshire. His involvement can be seen principally in two areas: causes which Surrey heard individually, and those causes determined by the earl and another councillor or councillors. In the first category, one can cite a dispute determined by Surrey in September 1492. It was a "... matier of variaunce for the imprisonment of Thomas Spycer, merchaunt, and Robert Deconson, tanner, citicins of this Citie [Yorke] which matier the day before Sheriff was at Ripele comond afor my lord of Surrey and ther by my lord it was determyned".[31] During the same year, Surrey examined Richard Hasilwad, a laborer, accused of causing the death of Richard Chapman, and as a result of his examination, the king issued Hasilwad a general pardon.[32] These examples indicate

[27] Reid, p. 504.
[28] Weever, p. 836.
[29] Thomas Stapleton (ed.), "Introduction", *Plumpton Correspondence. A Series Of Letters, Chiefly Domestick Written In The Reigns of Edward IV. Richard III. Henry VII. And Henry VIII.* (= *Camden Society*, 1st Ser., IV) (London, 1839), p. xcix and p. 96 of the text.
[30] *Ibid.*, p. 96.
[31] Raine, C III, 92.
[32] *C. P. R. 1485-94*, p. 423.

that Surrey could act sometimes individually in administering justice, making it probable that he had similar instructions to that of the Earl of Shrewsbury, who in 1522 as Lieutenant-General, was given authority to administer justice in all causes.[33]

Some causes, however, were settled by Surrey in conjunction with another councillor. An example of this type is the York City Council's request made in August 1490 to Surrey and Richard Tunstall to give their counsel regarding a matter of misconduct of the York masons.[34] Surrey's entry into this dispute originated from the request of the city's officials, but often his entry into disputes issued from a royal commission directed to him and other councillors there on the scene. An example of this is the inquiry directed by the crown into the death of Thomas Metcalf. As a result of the inquiry, John Heryson, who was accused of murdering Metcalf, was given a pardon. Heryson's innocence was certified "... by the earl of Surrey and other of the king's councillors staying on the spot and appointed to inquiry into the matter ...".[35] Another example is the commission issued to Thomas Rotherham, archbishop of York, Surrey; William Sever, the abbot of St. Mary's of York; Guy Fayrefax, a Yorkshire knight; and Richard Tunstall for the purpose of settling a dispute between the citizens of York and the prebendaries of St. Peter's cathedral in the city of York over a right of common pasture. The royal commission was issued in February 1490 and the matter appeared to be satisfactorily settled.

But the same old quarrel or a new one arose in 1494 to compel the attention of Surrey and his associate councillor, Sever, the abbot of St. Mary's. The two were appointed on Febuary 14, 1494 to inquire into a dispute between the city and the officials of the Minster or cathedral with authority given to Surrey and Sever to make examination of the disputants and send any they saw fit to the king's council.[36] The process of settlement in this interminable dispute is an interesting one and illustrates the interaction between justice on the regional and national levels. On the fourth of April, one day prior to a scheduled hearing before the earl and the abbot, the officials of York judiciously sent Surrey two pikes, two bremers, two eels, and twelve pence worth of mayn bread "... in consideracon of the gret payn and labour that he hath taken upon hym in that behalve ...".[37] Despite

[33] L. P., III, 2412.
[34] Raine, C III, p. 60.
[35] C. P. R. 1485-94, p. 332.
[36] Ibid., p. 320; Raine C III, 105.
[37] Ibid., p. 106.

the gift, no settlement was reached and in September Surrey wrote to the York city council "... for asmyche as by thexaminacon I have taken and hard in this behalve cannot set you at non accorde, therfore I charge you in the Kyngs name that accordyng to his high commaundement to me sent by his letters ye appoynt for you such persones as by you shalbe thought best within the Citie of York to appere before the Kyngs good grace and his Counsell nowe at the fest of halowemes next comying, for thansweryng and declaryng of your right and title concernyng the forsaid closing and hegging, for ye shall understand I have yeven like charge unto the forsaid vicars that they appoynt for theym suche persones as by thaym shalbe thought convenyent to appere afore the Kyngs highness at the said fest; at the which fest I purpose with Gods grace to be with the Kings highness and than I shall shewe and declare before his grace thexaminacon aforesaid and what I sawe and founde therin. ..."[38] Later in the month the York city council requested and received Surrey's permission to occupy the vicar's meadows as they had in the past. In October, Sever suggested that the vicars pay the York commons a yearly rent for the disputed area,[39] but this proved unacceptable to the officials of the various guilds who "... were acorded and determyned that thai wold have and use their etage and comon as well in the said Vicars leis [meadows] as thai had in other placez yerly duryng the tyme accustomed".[40] Not only was a valuable grazing area at stake here, but the guild members felt that the clergy were attempting to infringe upon one of their ancient rights. They became so hot-tempered that they openly defied the York city council's plea for moderation, and Surrey found it necessary to request the mayor and council to examine those who had uttered unsuitable language and to commit the same to prison. Though this was done, the matter was not closed, but merely increased in intensity with additional riots and further damage done to the Minster lees. [41] The situation was so serious that it prevented Surrey from making his proposed attendance on the king at the feast of All Hallows and from taking part in the festivities at Prince Henry's creation as Duke of York.[42] The king wrote on November 7, requiring the city officials to appear before him to answer for said riots. The York officials were worried by this royal summons and wrote on November 27, asking

[38] *Ibid.*, p. 107.
[39] *Ibid.*
[40] *Ibid.*, p. 108.
[41] *Ibid.*, pp. 108-12.
[42] *L. P. R III & H VII*, I, 402-04.

Surrey to certify their conduct to the king.[43] Thinking a letter insuf-
ficient, the officials decided to send George Kyrk, Charles Gray, John
Stockdale, Robert Plumpton, and John Custance as their representatives to see the earl with the intent of "... besechyng his lordship of
his best counsell and advice and that it wald please his lordship to
wrytt vnto the kyngs higyness for excusyng of the maier and there
cociticins...".[44] In reply on November 30, Surrey referred to the
official's similar appeal to Sever and the Dean of York, and the earl
told them that he would write on their behalf to the king. He offered
himself as surety for their good conduct and ordered them to appear
before the king on the eighth day of hillary term. Obligations for the
appearance of the York officials were to be drawn up before the
abbot and Surrey perceiving "... that this is bot a smalle matier for
me to cum over for to York therfor I wold ye shuld seale the forsaid
obligacons before my lord Abbot and delivere theyme vnto hyme in
my name".[45]

By December, the commons of the city of York had prepared themselves for submission to the king. At Greenwich on February 15, 1495
in the presence of Surrey and those York citizens summoned by privy
seals, the king reminded the citizens of the privileges of their ancient
city and advised them to take their legal causes to Surrey for his
assistance. Notwithstanding an appearance before the king, the disputants were not reconciled. In March, the York officials became so
incensed at the turn of events that they refused to go to processions
and sermons at the Minster. In April, Surrey offered to mediate: he
issued a temporary order to the officials to attend the processions at
the cathedral and invited Abbot Sever's aid in his deliberations. The
dispute was finally settled the following September when each party
agreed to enjoy jointly the commons of the vicars lees.[46]

Sever's part in settling the dispute between the corporation of the
city of York and the officials of the Minster has been cited by W. C.
Richardson as an example wherein Sever acted as President of the
Council of the North. Since Sever received bills of complaint and
petitions, examined witnesses, and advised arbitration, he reasons, as

[43]   Raine, CIII, 112.
[44]   York House Books, VII, fol. 122(v). Not printed by Raine.
[45]   Raine, CIII, 113.
[46]   *Ibid.*, pp. 113-123. Both Surrey and Sever were also involved in 1497 in an
attempt to settle a dispute between a Miles Willesthorpe, accused of enclosing a
portion of the York city common, by Sir William Gascoigne and other landowners.
Reid, pp. 81-82.

does Miss Rachel Reid, that Sever acted as president of the council during Surrey's lieutenancy.[47] But Surrey did the same and he was the King's Lieutenant in the North Parts. If anyone presided over the meetings of the Council of the North, he was the logical person to do it, not Sever. It may have been that any of the king's councillors in the North could receive petitions and initiate action for the settling of causes. It must be remembered that Surrey and Sever settled together the aforementioned dispute: it was not determined by Sever alone. Richardson neglects to mention Surrey's part in the proceedings. And one must note that Sever was a very important councillor slightly more accessible to the citizens of York through his residence at the abbey of St. Mary's than was Surrey who lived beyond the city at the royal castle of Sheriff Hutton. Ultimately, when Surrey left the North, the abbot became his successor as lieutenant and high commissioner in the north parts.[48]

From the meagre evidence presented one can draw few conclusions about Surrey's juridical activity. Minor and routine matters he handled by himself. Weightier matters that came to the attention of the king were usually provided for by specific commissions issued by the king to whom he saw fit, usually to Surrey and other important men of the North. The reference in one patent to the earl and other councillors on the spot indicates a conciliar approach to the determination of northern justice and northern problems, and reinforces the writer's belief, that, as in the time of Richard III, important matters were determined by the lieutenant or president and at least two councillors. Of course, the king could alter the procedure by issuing a commission to the lieutenant, individually, or to the lieutenant and one other councillor as he did in the dispute between the Minster and the corporation of York. There is little doubt that Surrey was assisted in ruling the North by prominent councillors of the king. Miss Reid acknowledges that Surrey had the assistance of Richard Tunstall, the steward of Knaresborough and Kendall and Abbot Sever, and that the earl had a council made up essentially of the stewards and constables of royal castles and lordships.[49] Thus, although Surrey was the chief officer of the king in the North, and by virtue of his office the presiding officer in any group of northern councillors, he shared

---

[47] W. C. Richardson, *Tudor Chamber Administration, 1485-1547* (Baton Rouge, La., 1952), pp. 135-36; Reid, pp. 78-79.
[48] *Ibid.*, p. 487.
[49] *Ibid.*, p. 78.

his civil authority with other members of the Council of the North.

Even in the military administration of the North, Henry VII emphasized conciliar activity. The most notable example of this emphasis is his placing the office of warden-general in commission during Prince Henry's youth. When Henry, the king's second son, was appointed warden-general of the marches on May 22, 1495 in place of Arthur, the office was to be executed in commission for him by Richard Fox, the bishop of Durham, William Tyler, captain of the city and castle of Berwick, and John Heryon de Ford, John Cartyngton, and Edward Ratcliff, Yorkshire worthies. Surrey was still, however, to be the deputy for the warden-general.[50] This policy was continued in 1500 when William Heron, Cartyngton, and Ratcliff were made commissioners and also deputies for the warden-general[51] since Surrey was no longer Lieutenant of the North. W. C. Richardson envisions a council in the North made up of the lieutenant and the important captains of the northern garrisons.[52] Thus, in military matters as well as in civil matters, the king's lieutenant was to be associated with and assisted by other of the king's men.

By virtue of his position as deputy warden-general of the marches, Surrey had important military powers, the most important of which was his power to array the men of Northumberland whenever Scotland threatened an attack. When Surrey was called upon to array all the able-bodied men between the Trent and the Tweed in 1495, his commission cited him as warden of the west and middle marches and not as lieutenant-general of the king's forces though he certainly was to be the English commander-in-chief. He was given the office of deputy warden-general to aid him in the execution of his military duties as King's Lieutenant of the North. The regular powers of a warden included treating with representatives of the Scottish king, maintaining peace on the borders, holding the warden's court on specified days, seeing that the marches under his jurisdiction were defencible, and arraying the men of the marches. As far as one can tell, Surrey was content to allow his duties to be performed by a deputy. This practice was not uncommon: Surrey's predecessor as deputy lieutenant in the east and middle marches, Robert Moulton,

---

[50] *Rot. Scot.*, II, 517-18.
[51] *C. P. R. 1494-1509*, p. 200. In another patent dated the same day, Ralph Grey is named with Ratclif and Cartyngton as commissioners. The name of Heron is omitted. *Ibid.*
[52] Richardson, p. 135.

had eight deputy substitutes plus eight warden sergeants to help him keep order in the marches.[53] In addition to his duties as deputy warden, Surrey had the keeping of the town and castle of Berwick, the most important northern outpost on the Anglo-Scottish frontier. Berwick had been taken from the Scots in 1482 and made into an English fortress. It and the fishgarths in the Eske estuary were the two chief objectives of Scottish military policy in the 1490's.

Though England and Scotland were at peace, the English were apprehensive about Scottish intentions.[54] The appearance of the impostor, Perkin Warbeck, who called himself Richard IV was cause for alarm. As early as 1493, Perkin had secured recognition at the court of Margaret of Burgundy: it was commonly rumoured that he would launch a continental invasion of England. The mayor of York alerted the city's citizens to their imminent danger and called upon them to do their duty. Henry VII commanded Surrey to call the men of York before him for the purpose of ordering the city's defense, and in August 1493 he made the earl responsible for defending all English territory north of the river Trent.[55] But no invasion from the continent materialized in 1493, and the English settled down to a policy of watchful waiting. The Scottish truce was renewed in 1494 to forestall any attempt on the part of Perkin to seek Scottish aid in securing the English crown. Despite this action, Perkin Warbeck was royally received and entertained at the Scottish court in November 1495. He was accepted as the legitimate king of England and given the hand of Lady Catherine Gordon in marriage.[56]

Henry's response to the danger presented by Perkin Warbeck's presence in Scotland was twofold: first, he pursued a policy of military preparedness in the North; second, he tried to preserve the Anglo-Scottish truce through diplomacy. On March 22, 1495 Surrey received a general commission to array all the able-bodied men living between the Trent and Tweed for defending the country against the Scots. At the same time, Richard Fox, the bishop of Durham and Lord Privy Seal received a commission of array for the palatinate of Durham, the county of Northumberland, and the lordships of Rydesdale and Tyndale. Specific commissions of array for the three ridings of Yorkshire were issued to Surrey, Ralph Neville, and other important northern

---

[53] P.R.O. C 82/60; P.R.O. C 71/107.
[54] Mackie, p. 137.
[55] Raine, CIII, 100-03.
[56] Mackie, pp. 137-38.

gentlemen in November.[57] Nor was diplomacy neglected: Henry VII wished to avert war at all costs. Surrey, Fox, William Sever, now bishop of Carlisle, Ralph Neville, lord Neville, Sir Thomas Dacre, and Sir William Tyler were commissioned to seek Scottish amity.[58] The English king hoped to seal Anglo-Scottish friendship by a marriage alliance: to this end, he offered James IV the hand of his eldest daughter, Margaret, then scarcely seven years old. He renewed his offer in 1496 and issued three separate commissions for this purpose. The commissioners named on May 5, 1496 were Fox, Sever and Surrey to whom were added Ralph Neville, Thomas Dacre, and William Tyler in the subsequent commissions dated June 23 and September 2. Any two of the commissioners had the power to act, but Fox had to be one of the two commissioners making the final treaty. It finally turned out that Fox, acting individually on the basis of a special commission, negotiated the marriage in 1499.[59]

Thus, there is the interesting spectacle of England preparing for war with Scotland on the one hand and trying to secure a lasting peace with her on the other. Open warfare came in 1496: the Scottish forces briefly crossed the Tweed on September 20, but hastily withdrew the following day. The Venetian ambassador, Antonio Spinola, was informed by his English correspondent that the Scots had taken the field, and he was also assured that the mustering of English forces by Surrey and Fox would easily dispose of any Scottish threat.[60] In January of the new year, Henry VII decreed that all Scots should leave England by the Feast of the Purification[61] (February 2). Surrey himself went north to Alnwich to inspect the state of border defences, then audaciously crossed the frontier, made a winter raid into the Scottish county of Tyndale, burned houses there, and laid waste the county.[62] The Scottish raid and English reprisal dampened what little

[57] C. P. R. 1494-1509, pp. 32, 52.
[58] William Hutchinson, The History and Antiquities Of The County Palatine, of Durham, 3 vols. (New Castle, 1785-94), I, 373. Hereafter cited as Hutchinson. Hutchinson errs when he speaks of a William, earl of Carlisle; he meant William, the bishop of Carlisle.
[59] Mackie, p. 157; C. D. R. Scot., 1622; Rot. Scot., II, 520-22. There were two commissions dated June 23, 1496 and one of them names John Cartyngton and Christopher Moresly in addition to the above named commissioners.
[60] Mackie, 140; C. S. P. Ven., III, 1478.
[61] Robert Steele, A Bibliography Of Royal Proclamations Of The Tudor And Stuart Sovereigns And Of Others Published Under Authority 1485-1714 With An Historical Essay On Their Origin And Use, 2 vols. (Oxford, 1910), I, no. 24 C.
[62] Weever, p. 836.

hope there was for securing a lasting peace between the two countries, and it is little wonder then that James IV could dismiss and disavow Perkin Warbeck and yet plan to make war on England.

Originally Henry VII had planned to send his trusted councillor and general, Giles Dawbeney, north with a large army to meet the Scots, but internal problems decreed otherwise. Dawbeney was diverted with his men to put down the Cornish uprising of June 1497, and then in the early autumn, to track down the hapless Perkin Warbeck, who attempted to stage an uprising of his own in Cornwall. Dawbeney never went North. Thus, Surrey became commander of the northern troops who resisted James IV and his force. As usual, Scottish timing was excellent. While Henry VII and Dawbeney were occupied with affairs in Cornwall, the Scots struck in late July. James IV and his troops crossed the border and besieged Norham Castle, which maintained a stout resistance for fifteen days until Surrey and Bishop Fox came to its relief. When James heard that Surrey was coming with a large English force, he fled to Scotland with the earl in close pursuit. Surrey followed up his advantage by going into Scotland where he brazenly assaulted and captured Ayton Castle in full view of James IV who was less than a mile away.[63]

Soon the idle Scottish king sent his Lyon-Herald to Surrey with an offer of battle. With alacrity the earl agreed to set terms for the battle, but James IV was not really interested in fighting a large scale engagement; therefore, he instructed his herald to request that Surrey and he settle the issue by hand-to-hand combat; the earl to receive a king's ranson should he prove victorious, and James to get Berwick and fishgarths should he win. Surrey was too astute a politician and general to take the offer seriously. He chided the king for his condescension in being willing to fight a lowly earl, and he held fast to his original commission, which was to do as much damage as possible to James IV and his forces. Surrey said he never would relinquish Berwick or the English rights to the fishgarths, but gallantly told the chivalrous king that he would, indeed, be happy to fight with him on horseback or on foot when his present commission was done.[64] After a stay of six or seven days in Scotland in the worst weather imaginable, Surrey withdrew to Berwick, disbanded his men, and awaited further instruction from his master, Henry VII.

[63] Mackie, pp. 140-47; Hutchinson, III, 402: *Hall's Chronicle*, pp. 480-81.
[64] Weever, pp. 836-37.

Surrey's retreat has been attributed to both inclement weather and lack of supplies,[65] but there is another factor to be considered — Henry VII's diplomacy. In a volume published by the Naval Records Society, M. Oppenheim asserts that Henry VII's secret diplomacy was the decisive reason behind Surrey's withdrawal. Certainly Surrey had enough munitions for a large scale military offensive, and the number of men accompanying him indicates such an offensive. Obviously the results of his summer campaign were not commensurate with the preparations made. In viewing the earl's military activity, which was confined to an eight mile radius of Berwick, Oppenheim surmises that Surrey deliberately wasted time by attacking inconsequential military objectives so that Henry's diplomacy could mature.[66] When one considers that Surrey was a party to the peace negotiations of 1495 and also actively engaged in the Anglo-Scottish marriage negotiations, one must conclude that Surrey knew what Henry wished. The only tangible result of Surrey's military adventure was the forcing back of the Scottish troops to Scotland. Then, too, Surrey may have derived some personal satisfaction from knighting his two eldest sons, Thomas and Edward,[67] who had participated in the campaign.

Henry VII was never averse to solving military problems by diplomacy. He had given Fox secret instructions relative to Scotland on July 5, 1497 and on the ninth gave Surrey, Thomas Darcy, William Tyler, Richard Cholmeley, and John Cartyngton a commission for forming a perpetual peace between the two countries.[68] Therefore, Surrey was conducting a war against the Scots, while he shared in a commission to treat for peace with them. Peace was not long in coming: the Truce of Ayton was concluded by the commissioners of each country on September 30. The truce was originally scheduled to last for seven years, but it was extended in 1499 to last until one year after the death of whichever king lived longer.[69] Thus, peace came to the northern borders, a peace that was soon be cemented by the marriage of Margaret Tudor to James IV.

Surrey's stay in the North was rapidly drawing to a close. In March 1498 he helped to expedite the collection of the subsidy from the city

[65] *Hall's Chronicle*, p. 482; Polydore Vergil, p. 101.
[66] M. Oppenheim (ed.), "Introduction", *Naval Accounts and Inventories Of The Reign Of Henry VII 1485-8 And 1495-7* (= *Navy Records Society*, VIII) (London, 1896), pp. xlvi-xlvii.
[67] Walter C. Metcalfe, *A Book Of Knights* ... (London, 1885), p. 31.
[68] *Rot. Scot.*, II, 530-31.
[69] Mackie, pp. 147-48.

of York.[70] The new wardens of the east and middle marches, Ralph Grey and William Heron, respectively, assumed their offices from the summer of 1499.[71] Surrey's last ties as a resident Lieutenant of the North were cut in 1500 when his offices of constable and steward of Sheriff Hutton were conferred on Thomas Darcy.[72] Actually, the earl was away from the North for a part of 1499 when he was at court. During that year he attended the trials of the little Earl of Warwick and Perkin Warbeck, who were accused of treason, convicted, and subsequently executed.[73] With the Scottish danger over and the northern area at peace, there was no further need of Surrey's continuous presence in the North, and the earl now took his place as one of the select councillors in Henry VII's inner ring.

Originally, Surrey went north to restore civil order in Yorkshire. Riots and other civil disorders kept him in the North longer than was expected. As a matter of fact, Surrey fully expected to participate in Henry's campaign in France in 1492, but the earl had to content himself with staying in England as one of those entrusted with the safe-keeping of Henry's realm.[74] His temporary stay lengthened into a ten year tour of duty as Lieutenant of the North as the North moved from crisis to crisis. Though the threat of civil disturbance was lessened after 1492, the Scottish peril required the earl's presence. The possibility of a combination of northern rebellion in favor of Perkin Warbeck and a simultaneous attack by the Scots was unsettling. The chief characteristic of his administration was his association with other councillors in carrying out his civil and military duties. There is no evidence to indicate that he used his warden's power to array the men of Northumberland. Usually specific commissions of array were issued to him alone and to him in conjunction with prominent men of the North to meet specific emergencies as was the case in 1495. In the great campaign of 1497 he was joined by Bishop Fox,

---

[70] Raine, CIII, 136.
[71] *C. P. R. 1495-1509*, p. 202.
[72] *Ibid.*, p. 203.
[73] C. G. Bayne and William Huse Dunham, Jr. (eds.), *Select Cases In The Council Of Henry VII* (= *Selden Society*, Vol., 75, for 1956) (London, 1958), p. 32. Hereafter cited as Bayne.
[74] Weever, p. 836. Surrey along with Sever, Tunstall, Henry Wentworth, Nicholas Knyfton and John Beverley were commissioned to collect funds in 1491 for Henry's expedition against France. *C. P. R. 1485-94*, p. 366. The career of Wentworth, the steward of Knaresborough Castle and a member of Surrey's northern council, is quite interesting. He originally came from Suffolk, but had specific orders to remain in the North. *Plumpton Correspondence*, pp. 94-95.

and in his most important judicial and administrative activities he was assisted by Sever and Tunstall. Henry's handling of the northern problem during Surrey's tenure as lieutenant shows an affinity for a conciliar type of administration and a reliance on the use of old, ready-made constitutional instruments, i.e. the office of the warden, the commission of peace, and commissions of oyer and terminer. Surrey's successors to his office, William Sever and Thomas Savage, the Archbishop of York, may each be considered as the King's Lieutenant and High Commissioner in the North Parts, but they did not have as ample powers as the earl, since neither held office as warden or Justice of the Forests beyond the Trent.[75] Surrey occupied a unique position in the history of the North and he uniquely discharged his civil and military functions as Lieutenant of the North. During the reign of Henry VIII, that king would look back to Surrey's tenure as Lieutenant for precedents in handling the northern problem until, in 1537, he eventually instituted the office of resident president of the council in the North.

There were distinct advantages in having Surrey as Lieutenant of the North. Unlike the great northern magnates, Surrey had no land holdings there. He could not combine a regional influence with his special constitutional powers to make himself a threat to the authority of the crown, as it might have been possible for a Percy or a Neville to do. Surrey was the king's creature, wholly dependent on him for sustenance and advancement. The earl had all the necessary qualities to fill his position brilliantly, yet he had none of the disloyalty and disaffection which could prove so dangerous if entertained by a powerful local magnate. Moreover, Surrey's northern employment solved the problem of what to do with this impoverished nobleman. When he emerged from the Tower early in 1489, he was only restored to the lands he held with his wife. It was not until 1492 that he was restored to his father's property and also received a new patent for the earldom of Surrey, which entitled him to obtain the customary annual £20 fee from the hanaper.[76]

Fees from his offices and income from land rented from the king provided the earl with a small income. As constable and steward of Sheriff Hutton, Surrey received £10 annually, one hundred shillings per office.[77] While at Sheriff Hutton, Surrey had the privilege of

[75]   Reid, p. 487.
[76]   Bodleian Ashmole Ms. 841.
[77]   Payments to Surrey as constable and steward of Sheriff Hutton begin in 1489

pasturing his animals below the park, a right formerly held by Henry VII's wife, Queen Elizabeth, for which the earl paid an annual rent of £6 13s 4d. In addition, he held a park there worth 60s per annum[78] and had the rent of four closes called Dalbyhorn, Saybyhirsh, Malinghern, and the Great Close, which together were worth £19 a year.[79] The earl was expected to maintain himself and his retinue from the use of the land and from a sum set aside by the king for this purpose, most likely in the neighborhood of one thousand marks a year.[80] Fortunately, offices such as porter of the castle and keeper of the park were royal appointments paid for out of the issues of certain properties and not paid for out of Surrey's pocket. The expense of holding the court of the lordship was also provided for by the king;[81] thus, the earl need only concern himself with the expenses of his personal staff. There is no record that Surrey received any special fee as Lieutenant of the North. Of course, he did receive a special contribution from the king for the maintenance of his retinue, and this allowance was probably augmented when he took the field against the Scots.[82] Although he was not paid specifically as the deputy warden-general of the marches, he was on occasion paid as the lieutenant of the east and middle marches and keeper of the west march. The usual fee was one hundred marks per march.[83]

---

when payment was made jointly to him and Ralph Bigod, the former constable and steward. After 1489 the earl was the sole recipient of the fees for these offices. P.R.O. DL 29/10512, 10515.

[78]   P.R.O. DL 29/10512, 10513, 10514, 10515.

[79]   These closes were granted to Surrey by Richard Cholmeley, the king's receiver general and John Dawney, Cholmeley's deputy. P.R.O. DL 29/10512, 10513.

[80]   This is the sum that the Earl of Shrewsbury received for his diet when he was Lieutenant General of the North in 1522. L. P. III, 2412. It seems likely that Surrey received the same amount during his tenure as King's Lieutenant. Although I can find no evidence of regular payments to Surrey for the maintenance of his retinue, there are two entries in the Tellers Rolls which seem to indicate some arrangement was made for the maintenance of his retinue. One on the Michaelmas 5H7 roll refers to a sum of £260 paid to the earl, whereas the other on the Easter 12H7 roll notes a payment of £418 14s 9d to Surrey for wages and maintaining his retinue. P.R.O. E 405 (2)/78, 79. If one can assume that similar payments were made during the years of Surrey's lieutenancy, the annual outlay would be roughly equivalent to the one thousand marks.

[81]   P.R.O. DL 29/10514.

[82]   L. P., III, 2412.

[83]   Usually the east and middle marches were joined under the wardenship of one man though Surrey was on occasion paid separately as warden of the middle march, and an individual appointment was made in 1500 of William Heron as warden of the middle march. P.R.O. E 405 (2)/77, 78; C. P. R. 1495-1509, p. 202. The entries in the Tellers Rolls do not seem to be complete with respect to pay-

For the greater part of his stay in the North, Surrey confined his activity to the vicinity of Yorkshire, and except for a brief period in 1495, he seems to have been in continuous residence at Sheriff Hutton. During February 1495 he attended the marriage of his eldest son, Thomas, to Ann Plantagenet, daughter of Edward IV and sister to Henry VII's queen. The Howard fortunes were on the mend. By the marriage settlement worked out between Surrey and Queen Elizabeth, the newly married couple were amply provided for.[84] In the preceding year, Surrey had been successful in purchasing the magnificent property of the borough of Bramber in Sussex, together with its castle, honor, and lordship. The property had been granted to Thomas West, lord de la Ware, on the attainder of Surrey's father John, duke of Norfolk, and was then in September 1494 conveyed to the earl for a pecuniary consideration of 500 marks at the specific request of Henry VII.[85]

With the conclusion of Surrey's duties as Lieutenant of the North, it is appropriate to take stock of the earl and the nature of his relationship with his king. The earl was then fifty-six years old, still vigorous, and in excellent health. If his appearance was anything like that of his eldest son, he had a short, thin, wiry build.[86] One portrait of the earl depicts him praying just before the battle of Flodden. At that time he was seventy years old, but still able to perform valuable service for the Tudors. The portrait presents a man with a spare, clean-shaven face, surrounded by thinning hair which fell to his shoulders and was cut in bangs across his forehead. There is a

---

ments to Surrey for his fees as warden. No list of Surrey's offices and fees would be complete without mentioning his purchase of the office of controller of works from Roger Hopton in February 1496. The office brought annual wages of £28 7s 6d. *C. C. R. 1485-1500*, 1209.

[84] Thomas Howard, junior, and his wife were to have the use of certain manors on the death of the Mowbray dowager duchess of Norfolk (Elizabeth d. 1507) and in addition, Thomas Howard, senior, was to give them the use of the manors of Lopham in Norfolk, Willington in Bedford, Prytewell in Essex, and Stoke in Sussex. In consideration of his giving up these manors, Surrey received an annuity of £120. Until the Mowbray properties became available, the Queen promised to provide for her sister's apparel. Thomas Madox, *Formulare Anglicanum* (London, 1702), p. 109. See also *Rot. Parl.*, VI, 479 for a list of the towns from which Surrey was to derive this revenue. During January of 1495 he participated in a commission of oyer and terminer for the city and suburbs of London. *C. P. R. 1494-1509*, p. 29. This was probably the commission that heard and gave judgment on the treasonable acts of William Stanley, the king's lord steward, who was subsequently executed.

[85] Madox, p. 212; *C. C. R. 1485-1500*, 824.

[86] *C. S. P. Ven.*, IV, 694.

pronounced resemblance to his father, John Howard, in his acquiline nose and large luminous eyes. His features are not so full or as attractive as those which give his father's countenance a bluff, good-natured air.[87] The earl had unusual vitality for his age and this is the key to his continued activity as a royal servant.

His tenure as Lieutenant of the North shows his involvement with Tudor administration on the regional level and indicates Henry's growing confidence in him. Ten years of efficient service as the king's deputy proved that the king's trust had not been misplaced. Their relationship during this period can be made the basis for several deductions about the character of each man and, particularly, Henry's conception of his role as king. The conviction that Surrey was a conservative political realist is reinforced by the examination of his conduct during this critical decade. The earl was content to ascend the path to royal favor by the steps dictated by Henry, rather than to support the flimsy military enterprise of Perkin Warbeck. Surrey's support of his king is indicative of the loyalty that Henry could command from his chief subjects and demonstrates the crown's new-found strength. Henry was not afraid of Surrey or his popularity, though he discreetly kept him at a northern post far from his native East Anglia. If he feared the earl, he would have kept him in prison. Above all, Henry's use of Surrey is illustrative of his reliance on capable ministers. As Francis Bacon said, the king "... was not afraid of an able man, as Lewis the Eleventh [of France] was; but contrariwise, he was served by the ablest men that were to be found; without which his affairs could not have prospered as they did".[88] In his efforts to spread the rule of law over his realm, Henry determined that his chief officials should be selected from the best men available. Henry realized that the law of the land cannot be operative unless order is first established: that is why he appointed Surrey Lieutenant of the North and gave him extensive military, administrative, and judicial powers.

While he was in the North, both his step-mother, Margaret Howard,[89] and his first wife, Elizabeth, died. Within several months of his wife's death the earl remarried, marrying Agnes Tylney, related in the

---

[87]   See Figures 1 and 2, facing p. 21 and 105 respectively.
[88]   Bacon, *Henry VII*, p. 476.
[89]   Margaret Howard died sometime before December 3, 1494 and bequeathed to Surrey, the supervisor of her will, a gold cup and a cross gilt with silver and gold. *Test*. Vet., I, 404.

second degree to his first wife, on November 8, 1497 in the chapel at Sheriff Hutton. His first wife left her property to John Bourchier, lord Berners,[90] the famous translator of Froissart, who was Surrey's brother-in-law by virtue of marrying Surrey's half-sister, Margaret. Little is known about Elizabeth Tylney, Surrey's first wife; Surrey had married her for political advantage when the Howards were just becoming politically important in Suffolk. No scandal ever touched her, and by John Skelton's testimony she was an august personnage. In fact, she was one of his patrons before he became tutor to young prince Henry.[91] She was survived by three sons: Thomas, Edward, and Edmund, and two daughters: Elizabeth and Muriel, and became by their efforts the antecedent of two English queens, Anne Boleyn and her daughter, the great Queen Elizabeth I, ond one queen consort, Catherine Howard.

[90] His first wife died in April 1497. *C. I. P. M. for H VII*, II, no. 18. Surrey received a special dispensation to marry from Pope Alexander VI since his new wife was within the prohibited degrees of the blood and because the banns of marriage were only published once. *Testamenta Eboracensia: A Selection Of Wills From The Registry At York* (= *Surtees Soc.*, XLV, for 1864) (Durham, 1865), p. 360. Hereafter cited as *Test. Ebor.*

[91] The relationship between Skelton and the Howards will be pursued in a future book. It is my present belief that Skelton's patroness was not Elizabeth Stafford, the second wife of his son Thomas, but Surrey's first wife Elizabeth. Most of the evidence concerns the dating of the poem, *The Garland of Laurel*, usually ascribed to Skelton's later period; but on the basis of new astronomical evidence — first cited in W. D. Stahlman and Owen Gingerich, *Solar And Planetary Longitudes For Years — 2500 to 2000 by 10-Day Intervals* (Madison, Wis., 1963) — which produces a date of May 8, 1495 as a possible composition date, I believe that the Countess of Surrey referred to by Skelton is Surrey's wife, not his son's.

IV

KING'S COUNCILLOR

Surrey's service as Lieutenant of the North illustrates Francis Bacon's saying that kings who "... have able men of their nobility shall find ease in employing them, and a better slide into their business, for people naturally bend to them, as born in some sort to command".[1] Not only had the earl demonstrated his facility of command while in the North, but he had also competently handled his duties, thus vindicating the king's faith in him. From his position as a king's councillor on special assigment in the North, he now slipped easily into the routine of one of those councillors who followed the king about the English countryside from royal palace to royal palace, giving the king the benefit of his advice and participating in both policy making and administrative work. Within two years after his return, Henry made him Treasurer General of the Exchequer, an important post in which the earl's abilities could be fully utilized. Henry's use of Surrey appears to disprove the old notion that the king did not trust his nobles, gave them only honorific posts, and relied primarily on "new men" who owed their fortunes exclusively to him and not to inheritance. Of course, Surrey's patent of nobility only went back to 1483, and his reduced circumstances from 1489 on made him dependent on the king's largess. He was indeed the king's creature, and the bond which held him to his king was based on mutual need, fear, and perhaps, grudging respect. Bacon tells us that few men loved the king, some feared him, and many reverenced him,[2] and it is difficult to tell into which category the earl fell, but most likely it was fear. Though not starved into submission by the king during his imprisonment, the earl could not possibly have escaped the conviction then that the beginning of all wisdom was fear of his majesty.

[1] Francis Bacon, *Essays, Advancement Of Learning, New Atlantis, And Other Pieces*, ed. by Richard Foster Jones (New York, 1937), p. 39.
[2] Bacon, *Henry VII*, p. 476.

Therefore, the course of Surrey's service as one of Henry's councillors seems predictable: stolid, sedulous, and maybe servile. The description, however, does not measure the breadth nor the depth of his contribution; it merely indicates the fact that he performed his work in a satisfactory manner. His urge for independent power was constantly checked by his king, but the desire to influence, to advise and control the monarch through the medium of the royal council always remained, and though Thomas never achieved a position close to the king during the reign of Henry VII, the accession of Henry VIII presented an occasion for the earl to become chief councillor and even the possibility of turning himself into an *alter rex*. The subject of this chapter, then, is Surrey's attempt to dominate Henry VIII's council, and it must by necessity include a discussion of his activity as a councillor under both kings, since his employment by the father prepared the way for his opportunity under the son.

Henry VII's council was omnicompetent. The few surviving records of conciliar meetings demonstrate that it handled domestic, diplomatic, and dynastic affairs. Such diverse matters as disputes between nobles, petitions of the Merchant Adventurers, foreign treaties, and royal marriages were on its agenda. Whatever concerned the king was the concern of his council.[3] Attendance was limited to those men, nobles, prelates, lawyers, and gentlemen, who had taken the special oath of a king's councillor. Since all councillors did not attend every meeting, it is necessary to distinguish between meetings of the group of councillors who formed a select inner ring of advisors and those meetings when most councillors were present. The term "whole council" has been applied to describe meetings of the latter type, and in them, the king was usually seeking greater participation in the decision making and adoption of his policies than could be obtained from his immediate circle of councillors. Of course, the whole council was dominated by the intimate councillors, especially the three great officers of state, the Lord Chancellor, Lord Treasurer, and Lord Privy Seal, who had the best record of attendance at meetings. Only Wolsey, Warham, and Morton, as Lord Chancellors, went to more meetings than Surrey, the Lord Treasurer.[4]

[3] For a complete discussion of matters dealt with by Henry's council see C. G. Bayne and William Huse Dunham, Jr. (eds.), "Introduction", *Select Cases In The Council Of Henry VII* (= *Selden Society*, No. 75) (London, 1958). For a good introduction to conciliar activity see S. T. Bindoff, *Tudor England* (Harmondsworth, Middlesex, 1950), pp. 58-63.

[4] Bayne, "Introduction", pp. xxxvi-xxxvii; William Huse Dunham, Jr., "The

But it is really the group of Henry's intimate councillors which is of interest here. Surrey, along with Morton, Alcock, Fox, Lovell, Empson, Dudley, Dynham, and Somerset were the important members of the council. With the exception of Surrey, no great nobleman was allowed into this select inner circle,[5] though nobles were still employed as Henry's generals and admirals. Since Henry did not go to war very often, it was rarely possible to use military prowess as a stepping stone to political prominence. Again, Thomas, earl of Surrey, was the exception which proves this rule. The king shied away from the use of nobles, partly from his aversion to allowing them to think themselves greater than they really were and thus, to be tempted into revolt, and partly because his custom was the use of clerks and men of lower degree for weighty affairs of state. It was not only politically advantageous to employ them rather than noblemen, but it was also more economical. Bacon notes the enormous pleasure which Henry derived from using clerics, whom he was able to reward from the revenues of the church and not from his own pocket, and the king's intense satisfaction that he could advance them by steps from the poorer paying bishoprics to the higher.[6] Presumably, the gentry also came cheaper than the nobility. To stress, however, only the political difficulty in the use of the nobility and the economic gain in the utilization of the other estates is to ignore the primary reason for a man's selection as a councillor: his ability. All of Henry's intimate councillors were able.

Not only were they able, but they were also ruthlessly efficient. Empson, Dudley, Fox, and Morton are the names of but a few and the most important councillors who earned the hatred of their countrymen for being so callous in the discharge of their duty to the king.

Members of Henry VIII's Whole Council, 1509-1527", E. H. R., LIX (1944), 187-210. For a detailed examination of Surrey's attendance and other activities see footnote 13 below. See also William Huse Dunham, Jr., who comments on the "whole council" in "Wolsey's Rule Of The King's Whole Council", A. H. R., XLIX (1943-44), 644-62.

[5] It has often been thought that John de Vere, the earl of Oxford and Lord Admiral, was an important councillor, but Pollard has shown that this misconception has arisen from confusing this nobleman with Sir Charles Somerset. Somerset was Chamberlain of the Household whereas Oxford was the Lord Great Chamberlain. Gladys Temperley, Henry VII (Boston-New York, 1914), p. 247; A. F. Pollard (ed.), The Reign Of Henry VII From Contemporary Sources, 3 vols. (London, 1913-14), I, xxvii-xxviii.

[6] Bacon, Henry VII, p. 318.

Had Empson and Dudley been less efficient instruments of their master they would not have lost their heads under Henry VIII, who ordered their execution to court favor with the multitude. Bishop Fox merited special attention from the Scottish poet Alexander Barclay as he stopped amidst a general indictment of the evils of court life to speak disparagingly of one of Henry VII's most trusted ministers.[7] And Cardinal Morton, Henry's chancellor, will be most often remembered in English History, not for his service to the state, but for the invention of "Morton's fork" wherein both the indigent and wealthy English were caught on the horns of a financial dilemma. The efficiency of Henry's cohorts was coupled with secrecy, for both the master and his servant's actions were clothed in mystery that disturbed and, at times, terrified sixteenth century Englishmen. Morton and Fox will not be thought of primarily in terms of their religious and educational benefactions, but more often as those "vigilant men, and secret",[8] agents of their dark prince.

Fox, who became Surrey's principal antagonist during the reign of Henry VIII was an ideal royal servant. Like his sovereign Henry VII, he was tight-lipped, had a head for finance — at least he operated on the same premise as his master, that income must exceed outgo, and was fanatically devoted to the king. He had shared the rigors of the invasion in 1485, started his service as the king's private secretary and risen to the office of Lord Privy Seal. Along the way he obtained the bishoprics of Exeter, Bath and Wells, Durham and Winchester, which he held until death.[9] His was a devotion born of admiration which sprang from close contact and mutual interests and ideals. Thomas More tells a very revealing tale about the extent of Bishop Fox's fidelity to Henry. During the parliament of 1504, More, as a burgess, stoutly and vociferously refused Henry's demands for a large subsidy. So eloquently and well did the future chancellor argue, that parliament refused to grant the special tax, and thus, the king's will was frustrated. So it was that More earned the indignation and ire of both Henry and Henry's minister, Bistop Fox. When it chanced that More had to make special suit to Fox, the bishop hoped to repay More for

---

[7] "Introduction", *The Eclogues of Alexander Barclay*, ed. by Beatrice White (= E. E. T. S., *Orig. Ser.*, No. 175) (London, 1928), p. xxii. Hereafter cited as *Eclogues of Barclay*.

[8] Bacon, *Henry VII*, p. 318. Apparently the term Morton's fork originated with Bacon. *Ibid.*, p. 377. J. D. Mackie thinks the term is more applicable to Bishop Fox. Mackie, p. 232.

[9] *D. N. B.*, VII, 590-94.

his former disservice to the king. He pretended to grant the young man favor in order to win his confidence and a confession of his offence towards Henry. Not knowing that the bishop meant to trap him, More asked Fox's chaplain, a friend of his, for advice. The chaplain told More to beware of Fox: "For my Lord Bishop, my master", quoth he, "in order to serve the King's turn, would agree to his own father's death."[10] Lest this story be totally construed as evidence of Fox's hard-heartedness, one should also reflect that Henry must have had some unusual quality which made his servants respect his kingship and him in such a manner. The king inspired and commanded his councillor's loyalty by his personal actions and public performance of his royal duties. Despite his unprepossessing physical appearance, he was every inch a king.

Henry rewarded Fox's fidelity by his complete confidence, even to the extent of making him his most important councillor after the death of Cardinal Morton. Bacon described Fox as, "... not only a grave counsellor for war or peace, but also a good surveyor of works, and a good master of ceremonies, and any thing else that was fit for the active part, belonging to the service of the court or state of a great king."[11] In fact, Bacon's remark suggests that Fox was really Henry's first minister and that the striking contrast between Henry VII's reign, where supposedly the king rigidly ruled his council, and Henry VIII's reign, where a king and a minister were at the center of political activity, is not so pronounced as it first appears: the difference is one of degree and not of kind.

A considerable amount of power was exercised in Henry's council by an executive committee composed of the Lord Privy Seal, the Lord Chancellor, and the Lord Treasurer. These men, Fox, Surrey, and Thomas Warham, the new Lord Chancellor, acting as a committee, determined the order of business, set prices in England, and handled most of the administrative details of conciliar work. This executive clique was assisted by other councillors designated as assessors and managed any business not advisory in function. In particular, the committee handled parliamentary petitions and other petitions from towns and individuals. During Henry VIII's reign this committee was requested to oversee the organization of the king's household and was

[10] Mildred Campbell (ed.), *The Utopia Of Sir Thomas More including Roper's Life Of More And Letters Of More And His Daughter Margaret* (New York, 1947), p. 213.
[11] Bacon, *Henry VII*, p. 450.

very important as a policy making body during the first year of
Wolsey's service as chancellor.[12]

When one considers the vast amount of administrative detail done
by this committee, the work of Surrey as treasurer is put into new
perspective. Moreover, the evidence that Surrey was in constant
attendance as a councillor, and it must be noted that he missed only
two of the recorded council meetings for Henry VII and seven or eight
meetings under Henry VIII, shows that the Lord Treasurership was
an important office, for there is a sharp increase in Surrey's attendance
after his promotion in 1501 to the post of treasurer.[13] Whether his
presence was required by virtue of his office or by virtue of his
capacity as a special councillor to the king is a moot point. Normally,
one would expect the great officers of state to be present at meetings
of the whole council, and perhaps it is best to think of Surrey as a
councillor whose new office conferred additional duties and responsibilities which could only be met by continuous attendance.

[12] A. F. Pollard, *The Evolution Of Parliament*, 2nd ed. (London, 1926), p. 37;
A. F. Pollard, *Wolsey*, new ed. (London, 1953), p. 70; Jervis Wegg, *Richard Pace:
A Tudor Diplomatist* (London, 1932), p. 66; *L. P.*, I, 206. It was this committee
of Warham, Fox, and Surrey which received the articles for Catherine of Aragon's
marriage to Henry VIII. *L. P.*, V, 362.
[13] Surrey was originally appointed treasurer to serve as of June 16, 1501, and he
received reappointment under Henry VIII. His wages amounted to twenty shillings a day. *C. P. R. 1494-1509*, p. 239; *L. P.*, I, 138 (98). For record of payment
of this fee see P.R.O. E 405/82-83-84-85-86. Although Surrey missed two council
meetings in November 1504, he did attend other meetings in the same month.
Some of the matters discussed include business concerning the Merchant Adventurers and Merchant Taylors, the rebellion in Ireland, the reception of the Spanish ambassadors, and a variance between the Archbishop of Canterbury and the
Earl of Northumberland. Bayne, pp. 33-46. During the years 1503-04 Surrey was
quite busy. In 1503 he was steward at the trial of Edward Sutton, a knight
charged with a felony. *L. P. R III & H VII*, II, 379. On April 21, 1504 he
participated with other knights of the garter in a special ceremony. A. H. Thomas
and I. D. Thornley (eds.), *The Great Chronicle of London* (London, 1938), pp.
328-29. In July he was present when a treaty of amity was concluded with Spain.
Bayne, p. 37. In November, Surrey, Fox, Giles Daubeny, John and Thomas
Frowyk decided a variaunce in favor of Cicely, wife to the late Marquis of
Dorset, against her son Thomas. *C. C. R. H VII* (unbound volume in P.R.O.), 368.
Surrey's missed meetings under Henry VIII include: possibly October 14, 1509,
and for certain, June 19, July 8, 1510; May 8, 1511; May 28, 1516; January 25,
June 17, and October 11, 1518. In the case of six of the missed meetings, Surrey
did attend other council meetings in the same month. Huntington Library Ms.
El. 2655. I am grateful to the Huntington Library for permission to cite this
manuscript and to Prof. William Huse Dunham's article, "The Ellesmere Extracts
from the 'Acta Consilii' of King Henry VIII", *E. H. R.*, LVIII (1943), 301-18,
for bringing my attention to it.

One of his new duties as treasurer was to participate as a judge in the newly created court established by the act for star chamber of 1487. This court should not be confused with the famous Court of Star Chamber; the two are entirely different courts, having separate jurisdictions: the former being specifically limited to adjudicating in cases involving the offences of maintenance, embracery, retaining by indenture, the corrupt returning of juries, bribery, and riots; while the latter could deal with most cases except treason. The creation of this special court to handle specific offences is but one of the examples of Henry VII's willingness to innovate. By this act a panel of judges was created, consisting of the Lord Chancellor, the Lord Treasurer, the Lord Privy Seal, or any two of them; one bishop and one temporal lord; and two chief justices. The court was not, as Pollard thought, set-up especially to punish misconduct in the royal household — this was a new court of criminal jurisdiction. Eventually the court proved to be superfluous, since it found itself excercising a small portion of the same jurisdiction as the Court of Star Chamber and not performing with the same competence. Most of the cases dealt with were inconsequential and as time passed it became apparent that it was fulfilling no vital function.[14] Surrey's participation as a judge adds further weight to the idea that the post of treasurer was not unimportant, and, in this instance, shows that he was deeply involved in one of Henry VII's experiments in government.

In addition, Surrey had complete administrative control of the exchequer and also the authority to appoint minor officials in it and the customs service. For example, he appointed Henry Everard, his secretary, to the post of teller, and the earl usually signed the order of appointment for the escheators for the various counties.[15] Christopher Mitford, the customer or customs official in the city of Newcastle, originally bought his office from Surrey for £55 and then paid another twenty marks for obtaining letters patent which gave him legal title to his office.[16] If this illustration is typical of the way in which one procured a customs post, and it seems to be, then Surrey was a man of great influence and the recipient of all the advantages which normally accrue to the chief of a great patronage system. Even Wolsey at the height of his power dared not invade Surrey's special sphere, and so it is not surprising to find Richard Pace writing to

[14] Bayne, "Introduction", pp. li-lxxii.
[15] L. P., I, 2008, 2484 (17), 2617 (17), 2772 (4), 2829.
[16] L. P., IV, 959.

Wolsey, requesting that he speak to Surrey on behalf of an Irishman, Mr. Wise, for a customs post at Bristol.[17]

As treasurer of the exchequer, the earl was also concerned with his country's trade. Special licenses to import various stuffs, such as cloth of gold, were signed by the treasurer, and he made the arrangements for the conduct of England's annual wool fleet to the Staple at Calais.[18] Though he seldom handled financial matters personally, he could on occasion do so and there is record of a request by Sir Charles Somerset, the chamberlain of the chamber, to have Surrey pay four yeomen the "fee of the corone".[19] Presumably, Surrey complied with the request. In addition, the earl as head of the exchequer received petitions dealing with financial matters, since the exchequer had special jurisdiction in cases involving debtors to the crown. Of course, the barons of the exchequer actually tried the cases and Surrey's connection seems to have been administrative. In fact, his position was largely administrative and the references made to him in Henry VII's will as Treasurer General confirm this.[20]

As Treasurer General, Surrey did not have as much to do with the kingdom's finances as did treasurers in the fourteenth and fifteenth centuries. There are two reasons for this state of affairs: the first is the increasing importance of the financial operations conducted by the Treasurer of the Chamber at the expense of the exchequer; and the second is the tendency of the under-treasurer in the exchequer to handle routine financial matters formerly handled by the Treasurer General. The concentration of financial activity under Henry VII in the chamber is a well-known story and is often cited as evidence of Henry's success in exercising almost personal control over the nation's finances. It was much easier and quicker for the king to work through his household treasury than through the complicated machinery of the exchequer which badly needed modernization. Throughout his reign Henry increased the financial responsibility of the chamber, while decreasing that of the exchequer.[21] Since parliament seldom met

---

[17] L. P., II, 4275.

[18] L. P., I, 1940, 2211; L. P., III, 2214 (20).

[19] B. M. Egerton 2603, fol. 3 (r). This document has tentatively been dated as 1505. During this year Surrey was one of five men commissioned to collect one of Henry's benevolences. The other four were Thomas Lovel, Roger Lupton, John Oxbridge, and William Pawne. C. P. R. 1494-1509, p. 458. For another example of a payment made by Surrey see L. P. Addenda, I, 222.

[20] L. P., I, 1. An example of a petition to Surrey for remission of debt may be found in L. P. Addenda, I, 340.

[21] Arthur Percival Newton, "The King's Chamber under the Early Tudors",

during his reign — which meant fewer demands for subsidies usually collected by the exchequer, the financial business of the exchequer was further reduced. Henry's distate for the exchequer probably sprang from his dislike of an inefficient and cumbersome instrument and perhaps from the fear that it could become a useful weapon in the hands of a parliamentary opposition party.

Since most of the customs records were burnt in the great London fire of 1665,[22] we shall never be in a position to tell exactly how much authority over and interest in England's trading activities that the Treasurer General exercised. What little evidence there is seems to indicate that he was an important figure. This activity, plus his administrative and judicial responsibilities, noted above, must be considered when assessing the constitutional and political importance of Surrey's office. It no longer seems correct to say, as do Dr. G. R. Elton and Professor W. C. Richardson, that the office was a magnate office, that is an office with virtually no importance given to a high ranking noble as a sinecure.[23] Surrey did work at his job, and his political prominence, especially during the first few years of Henry VIII's reign, issues, at least in part, from holding the office of Treasurer General.

Not only was Surrey Henry's treasurer, but he was also one of Henry's diplomats. There was, of course, no diplomatic corps in Henry's day developed along the lines of present day diplomatic establishments. Though Henry VII used secret agents on occasion for gathering special information, he did not appear to have a network of resident ambassadors as did Spain and the chief Italian city-states.[24] Unless new evidence is revealed, one must believe that the true growth of English diplomacy comes with the use of Henry VIII's resident agents such as Antony Spinelly at the court of Margaret of Savoy and

---

E. H. R., XXXII (1917), 348-72. Henry VIII, too, was cognizant of the moribund state of exchequer and decided in 1519 to debate with his council the possibility of the exchequer reform. L. P., III, 576.

[22] Henry Atton and Henry Hurst Holland, "Preface", The King's Customs, 2 vols. (London, 1908-10), I, v.

[23] Richardson, p. 484; G. R. Elton, The Tudor Revolution In Government: Administrative Changes In The Reign Of Henry VIII (Cambridge, 1953), p. 22. Also see J. L. Kirby, "The Rise of the Under-Treasurer of the Exchequer", E. H. R., LXXII (1957), 666-67 and Frederick C. Dietz, English Government Finance 1485-1558 (= University of Illinois Studies in the Social Sciences, IX, no. 3) (Urbana, Ill., 1920), pp. 60-62.

[24] Garrett Mattingly, Renaissance Diplomacy (Boston, 1955), pp. 145-46.

William Knight at Ferdinand's court.[25] In Henry VII's time men were not the specialists in foreign service that they were to become in Elizabeth I's day. The usual practice was to select men from the council to conduct certain diplomatic negotiations. After receiving their instructions, they left England for the foreign country and remained in it until the negotiation was complete. Then they returned home.

Many of these negotiations concerned the important business of dynastic marriages, that is, the arrangement of marriages between the children of the leading European dynasties. The necessity of strengthening, if possible, and perpetuating his dynasty was the first and greatest responsibility of any king. He did this by seeing that both he and his children married suitable, healthty, and attractive princesses. Who the king or prince married was a grave political question to both his own countrymen and foreign princes. Quite naturally, the king's subjects worried about whether a new queen consort would tie her husband to her apron strings and rule the country by ruling her husband. If a king became too uxorious and the foreign interest of his wife were advanced at the expense of the country's, then there were certain to be public outcries and, in some cases, private plots to set things right. On the other hand, it was possible to seal diplomatic revolutions by a royal marriage between former enemies, as in the case of the marriage between Mary, Henry VIII's sister, and Louis XII of France. And the supreme achievement of dynastic marriages was, as the Hapsburgs demonstrated, to build a great empire through a series of fortunate marriages until a Charles V ruled Spain, the Low Countries, and the Germanies.

Henry VII knew the value of a good marriage, and his success in matchmaking laid the basis for the eventual union of Scotland and England. He had a master plan based on dynastic marriage for securing peace and for winning acceptance of England as a major power. He intended to have his first son, Arthur, marry Catherine of Aragon, the daughter of Ferdinand and Isabella of Spain; his first daughter, Margaret, marry James IV of Scotland; and his second daughter, Mary, marry Charles, the prince of Castile and heir to both Ferdinand and the Holy Roman Emperor Maximillian. Not only did Henry wish to win foreign acceptance of his dynasty, but he also hoped to solidify an Anglo-Spanish alliance and to detach, if possible, Scotland from France, her traditional ally and England's ancient enemy. In this

[25] *L. P.*, I, 568, 1101, 1239, 1327.

policy he was eminently successful, and his faithful servant Surrey aided in all the transactions.

The earl helped conclude the final details for Prince Arthur's marriage, and he was among those nobles who met Catherine at Ambresbury as she slowly made her way from Plymouth to London.[26] The pale, consumptive Arthur wed Catherine on November 14, 1501 at St. Paul's and after the festivities took her to live with him at Ludlow Castle, Shropshire. On April 2, 1502, less than five months later, Arthur died and it was Surrey's sad duty to journey to the Prince's castle and make his obsequies as chief mourner for the king.[27] Arthur's death was a national catastrophe. The sixteen year old lad had caught the fancy of the English nation: they admired him and looked to him for a peaceful succession to the throne, since he united in himself the blood of the rival houses of Lancaster and York. But he did not live to emulate the deeds of the legendary Arthur of the English; he was too frail to risk his body in the joust as did his more robust brother. The country, however, could comfort itself, even as the king comforted his queen, that prince Henry lived, and that a peaceful succession could still be accomplished through him.

Arthur's death momentarily clouded the king's plans for a matrimonial alliance with Spain. Prince Henry, not quite ten years old, was too young to marry Catherine, and even if such a marriage were proposed, it meant a period of waiting before the marriage could be solemnized. Henry would not reach the age of consent for another four years. Difficulties to such a match were envisioned on all sides. What would become of Catherine, and, more important to Henry VII, what would happen to the portion of her dowry which he had already received? According to the usual custom, half of Catherine's dowry had been delivered by the Spanish representatives when she married Arthur and the remainder was to have been delivered in the next year or two. Now that Arthur was dead, the Spanish government would not send any additional monies and requested that that portion which Henry had be returned. This he resolutely refused to do and kept both the girl and what money he had obtained. Catherine was in difficult straits and to make matters worse, she was not even allowed to see

---

[26] Garrett Mattingly, *Catherine Of Aragon* (Boston, 1941), pp. 34-35. Prof. Mattingly errs when he calls Surrey's wife the titular duchess of Norfolk. Surrey's wife did not become duchess until 1514 when Surrey became duke. Mattingly has confused Elizabeth Mowbray, the dowager duchess, with Surrey's wife.

[27] *D. N. B.*, I, 603; Mattingly, *Catherine Of Aragon*, pp. 48-49.

Prince Henry, who was kept under close surveillance by his father.[28] The story of the king's protracted negotiations over his second son's marriage with Catherine and the pitiful condition of Catherine as she waited, a virtual prisoner in England, are familiar tales and, though interesting, are not germane to our story. We must concern ourselves with another marriage alliance — that of James IV of Scotland and Margaret Tudor, in which Surrey played a key role, both in the preliminary marriage negotiations and the actual nuptial festivities.

In July of 1499, James had concluded a peace treaty with England. The following September, Bishop Fox was commissioned to negotiate a marriage alliance between the two countries and on October 8, 1501, Fox, Surrey, and Henry Dean, the Archbishop of Canterbury, received a commission to treat with James's ministers. By November 1502, final arrangements for the marriage and peace treaty had been worked out and ratifications of the treaties took place that December. According to the terms of the marriage agreement, Margaret was to be brought to Lamberton Kirk in Scotland by September 1, 1503, and the marriage would take place within fifteen days. The princess's dowry was set at the magnificent sum of 30,000 English gold nobles, 10,000 of which would be presented on her marriage day, and the remainder within two years.[29] Surrey was accorded the signal honor of being chosen chief commissioner to escort Margaret to Scotland.[30] The honor was not an empty one: it was a mark of the king's especial esteem and confidence in him. The king was selecting someone who could preside over Margaret's progress to Scotland in a manner befitting the occasion and to the princess's dignity. It was exactly the sort of assignment which the earl relished. He had the opportunity to exercise his authority in the matters of precedence that were so dear to the heart of every English nobleman, and he could display himself to advantage before the cheering throngs of simple Englishmen who wished to take a last look at their departing princess. These progresses of royalty and retinue parading through the English countryside were the food and drink which fed the medieval appetite for spectacle and color. Such ceremonies were all-important, and who participated and who led the progress were items of interest to all men, since these were one of the few tangible contacts which the lower classes had with royalty and its entourage. Hence, Surrey's

[28]   *Ibid.*, pp. 52-116.
[29]   *C. D. R. Scot.*, IV, 1655, 1658, 1676, 1678, 1693, 1695; *Rot. Scot.*, II, 550-55.
[30]   Weever, p. 837.

special commission was visible evidence of his political and personal association with the king.

The king himself took Margaret from Richmond to Margaret Beaufort's house at Collyweston, Northamptonshire. There he gave her to the care of Surrey and his wife, who were to be responsible for the princess until she arrived in Scotland. The princess's party left Collyweston on July 8, 1503 and by slow stages made its way to the North. Bells were rung and people turned out to see the princess as she went through Grantham, Newark, Tuxford, Sirousby, Doncaster, Pomfret, and York. At York the entourage was met by the Earl of Northumberland and a reception held there with Surrey arranging the precedence. Margaret was presented with a gift of a silver and gold piece which was emblazoned with the flag and arms of the city of York. After the mayor had made his presentation, Margaret graciously accepted it and then discreetly told Surrey to take it.[31] In riding out of the city there was a slight altercation between Sir William Conyers, the sheriff of York, and the mayor. Conyers lifted his rod toward the princess and the mayor admonished him that such was not his right within the liberty of the city, and Surrey ". . . herying these words and langagez emong theym commaunded theyn to sesse and said unto the said Sir William: Sir Shireff, putt down your rodde, ye do wrong to bere any within the libertiez of this Citie and then the said Sir William held down his rodde on lowe endelong by his horse syde unto he come beyonde Mawdeleyn chapell without the libertiez of this Citie, and then and there he toke up his rodde sayng, now Shireffs [of the city of York] hold down your rodds for it is within myn office; and they said so they wold and bad God spede hym."[32]

From York the procession went through Newbrough, Allerton, Darneton, and on to Durham where the party stopped for three days. After leaving Durham with the Earl of Northumberland still in their company, they proceeded to New Castle where Northumberland provided a sumptuous banquet. Then to Morpath, to Alnwich, and to Berwick where ordinance was discharged and the procession moved on its stately way to Lamberton Kirk where Surrey's company was met on August 1, 1503 by one thousand Scots. Margaret did not meet James until August third at Asquith Castle where the chivalrous prince wooed his bride-to-be bareheaded in the provencal manner, and the

[31] John Leland, *Antiquarrii De Rebvs Brittannicis Collectanea*, 2nd ed., 6 vols. (London, 1770), IV, 265-71; Mackie, p. 161; Raine, C III, 188.
[32] *Ibid.*, p. 189.

princess and Surrey's wife danced for the king. The next day was
spent at New Battle Castle and Surrey rode out to meet the king who
came with a small company of retainers. It was a festive, jolly day:
the king surprised Margaret playing cards, Lady Surrey and the
Princess danced, James played the lute and clavichord, and the
Scottish king even stole a kiss from Margaret. After saying adieu,
James displayed his physical prowess by vaulting into his horse's
saddle without putting foot to stirrup.

The king came at suppertime on the fifth, kissed Margaret, and
accepted from Surrey, Henry VII's gift of a splendid horse. The next
day Margaret danced for the assembled company and on the seventh
received James's gift of some palfreys. This same day she rode behind
the king through the city of Edinburgh in honor of her marriage which
was to take place there the next day. Both Surrey and his wife played
conspicuous parts in the wedding ceremony. Draped in a long gown
of cloth of gold, Surrey conducted the princess to the chapel of Holy-
roodhouse where his wife carried Margaret's train and the Archbishops
of Glasgow and York performed the marriage ceremony. After the
wedding mass, Surrey, Fox, and the two archbishops dined with
James at the first serving — Queen Margaret had to wait until the
second. No outdoor sports were planned for the day after the wedding,
and the guests amused themselves at the palace and went to mass.
As part of the palace entertainment that day, the Countess of Surrey
and her daughter, Lady Muriel Grey, cut the king's beard and for
this jest received fifteen ells of cloth of gold. On the tenth, eleventh,
and twelfth of August, jousts were held in the Queen's honor and on
Sunday, the thirteenth, Surrey, with the rest of the company, accompanied Margaret to mass, and here ends the story of Surrey's duties
to the new queen.[33]

Although weddings are usually occasions for recording the happi-
ness of bride and groom, Margaret was far from being as happy as
the proverbial bride should be. She felt hurt and angry because her
husband preferred Surrey's company to her own. She was furious,
and wrote bitterly to her father:

Sir, as for newys I have none to send, but that my lorde of Surrey ys yn
great favor with the King her that he cannott forber the companey off hym
no tym off the day. He and the bichopp off Murrey orderth every thyng
as nyght [nigh] as they can to the Kyngs pleasur. I pray God it may be for

[33] Leland, IV, 275-300; Mary A. E. Green, *Lives Of The Princesses Of England
From the Norman Conquest*, 6 vols. (London, 1857), IV, 94.

my por [poor] hartts ease in tyme to come. They calnot [call not] my Chamberlayne to them; whych I am sur wull speke better for my part than any off them that ben off that consell. And iff he speke any thyng for my cause my lord of Surrey hath such worrds unto hym that he dar speke no furder. God send me comford to hys pleasur, and that I and myne that ben lefftt her with me be well entretid such wayse as they have taken.[34]

The Scottish king loved this imperious old warrior, Surrey. As one knight to another, there was a strong bond of respect and affection between them, and far from disliking the earl for the harm he had done James while serving as Lieutenant of the North, the king loved him all the more. As Surrey's epitaph records, James told him that ". . . he loved hym the better for suche service as he had doon before to the Kyng his Father Kyng of England, thoughe the hurte war doon to hym, and to his Realme, and he gave to hym then at his departyng great gyfts."[35]

Laden with gifts, the earl took his leave of the Scottish king and queen and returned once more to the English court. He had carried out his duties on this mission in his usual efficient manner and gained the respect of the Scottish king in the process. From Margaret, however, Surrey earned something less than respect, for the affection which her husband lavished on his old enemy irritated her. After all, she should have been the center of attraction and not Surrey who was a mere soldier while she was a queen; and so she had written to her father. Though Henry VII's reply is unknown, the earl's position vis à vis the king remained unchanged, and he continued to serve as treasurer, councillor, and diplomat.

As early as the year 1500 Henry may have been thinking in terms of having his second daughter Mary marry Charles, the prince of Castile. During this year, Henry VII, accompanied by Surrey and a host of nobles and prelates, met Charles's father, Philip of Burgundy at Calais. As ruler of the Low Countries, which traded extensively with England, Philip was a valuable ally and a marriage alliance would reinforce their economic ties with that of a friendly, dynastic contract. Though it was not possible to complete the marriage negotiation during the lifetime of Philip, who died in 1506, serious attempts were made in 1507 and 1508 to do so. During November 1507, Surrey, along with Fox, Thomas Lord St. John, and Dr. Nicholas West, was sent to Flanders in order to construct the alliance. The following year,

[34] Henry Ellis, *Original Letters, Illustrative of English History*, 2nd ed., First Series, 3 vols. (London, 1825), I, 41. Hereafter cited as Ellis, *Letters*.
[35] Weever, p. 837.

Surrey; John Young, the master of the rolls; and a bright young clerk named Thomas Wolsey, the king's chaplain; were sent to Antwerp as emissaries to Prince Charles's grandfather and guardian, Maximilian; and further negotiations were conducted. Apparently the mission was successful, for in December of 1508, Surrey and many other nobles stood surety for a 50,000 crown bond for the marriage of Mary and Charles.[36] At the time of Henry's death in April 1509, Mary was contracted to marry Charles, but the marriage treaty was never honored due to a diplomatic revolution effected during the reign of Henry VIII.

When Henry VII died, England was at peace with the major European powers: France, Spain, and the Holy Roman Empire, and also with her northern enemy, Scotland. The king had served his country well, for not only had he kept his country out of war, but he had also eliminated the possibility of rebellion. He lived out his last few years undisturbed by the threat of foreign invasion and little concerned with the prospect of major uprisings. Great prosperity accompanied this era of tranquility, and Henry died the richest monarch in all Christendom. His policies of harsh justice at home and peace abroad insured a quiet and orderly succession to the throne. Though few men cared to shed a tear for the departed king, especially in view of the rising sun of Henry VIII, the old king was the real architect of the Tudor greatness. Without the firm foundations put in place by the first Tudor, the martial and marital exploits of the second Tudor would not have been possible. His twin achievements were making the succession of his son certain, that is, making his dynasty politically secure by ruthlessly hunting down and exterminating any possible claimants to the throne, and stabilizing the crown's finances by rigid economies and a more careful system of accounting.

The late king's funeral and preparations for the new king's coronation kept Surrey extremely busy during the months of May and June, 1509. On May tenth, Henry VII's body was brought from Richmond to St. Paul's and Surrey's son, Sir Edward Howard, the king's bannerer,

---

[36]   L. P. R III & H VII, I, 438-46, II, 87; James Gairdner (ed.), Historia Regis Henrici Septimi, A Bernardo Andrea Tholosate Conscripta; Necnon Alia Quaedam Ad Eundem Regem Spectantia. (London, 1858), pp. 100-03. The Manuscripts of the Corporations of Southampton and King's Lynn (London, Historical Manuscripts Commission, 1887), p. 113. The brunt of the negotiations apparently fell on Surrey and Young, for they spent fifty-seven days in embassy to the Emperor Maximillian. Surrey got forty shillings per day, while Young received thirteen shillings four pence per day. L. P., II, 1441. See also C. S. P. Span., I, 562-72.

carried the late king's banner and battle axe during the ceremony, performing the same service his grandfather had for Edward IV. Surrey as Lord Treasurer was among those who "... brake their staves and cast them into the grave ...".[37] The earl was also one of the executors of Henry VII's will and one of those designated to settle any accounts outstanding. He continued in his post as treasurer, kept his ties with the North, and was granted the office of earl marshal for the coronation, an office eventually given him for life. He was also one of the officials made responsible for settling the expenses of those taking part in the coronation.[38]

The glorious spectacle of an English coronation often takes the breath away of observers. The enthusiastic onlookers eagerly participate in the solemn ceremony in which the English nation willingly acknowledges a new lord and master. The nation accepts a popular new sovereign in return for the sovereign's affirmation before God and man that he will preserve the old rights and liberties and rule according to the laws of God. And in the midst of this ceremony was Surrey, duplicating the services his father had performed so many years before for Richard III. In Richard's time the Howard association with the sovereign was clouded in mystery and appeared to have its origins in the grossest of all possible political connivance, but in the time of Henry VIII their position was based on a right, not only the right of inheritance, but the right to the Tudor confidence grounded on years of faithful service.

Beneath the explosion of goodwill which hailed Henry VIII's coronation, there was reason for gladness. Many looked to the huge, handsome, auburn-haired king for a mitigation of the strict attention to business attitude of his father. They had had careful accounting and peaceful diplomacy from the father — now they looked for revels and martial exploits from the son. The contrast between father and son was marked: most people saw the youthful Henry as the embodiment of all kingly virtues and all desirable physical attributes, while the father impressed them as a miserly, old parvenu. They anticipated a new, golden era under the direction of a gentle, understanding prince who would seek only their true interests. But in

---

[37] L. P., I, 20.

[38] Ibid., 1, 81, 94 (88), 132 (98), 546 (42). During May 1509, the York city council wrote to Surrey requesting that he use his good offices with the new king, but he was too busy to give their emissary, William Chamerleyn, anything but loving words and the assurance that he would do "... the best he can for this Cite". Raine, CVI, 27-28.

addition to the hopes and golden visions of the future, the people could congratulate themselves that the treasury was full, the diplomatic scene fairly stable, and many of Henry VII's trained councillors available for duty with the new king.

With Henry VIII's accession came Surrey's opportunity to rule the king's council. The king was young, inexperienced, only recently married, and probably, in the eyes of his councillors, not yet aware of his royal responsibilities. What better chance for an elder statesman such as Surrey to step in and take the burdens of government away from a light-hearted and light-headed youth. In fact, what was to prevent Surrey from completely dominating the council and from becoming an *alter rex*? He had many qualifications for such a role: his proven loyalty to the Tudor dynasty, his understanding of the administrative machinery of English government, his wide experience as a councillor, judge, treasurer, and diplomat, and a distinguished military career which especially fitted him to advise a young prince who lived by the warrior's code. On the debit side of the ledger, the earl, who was remotely descended from the Plantagenets, was sixty-six years old and an important nobleman who moved closer to the throne with each successive execution of the Tudor rivals. His age need not be a handicap if he had sufficient vigor of mind and body, and the boundless energy necessary to keep up with an active, over-athletic prince. His nobility, far from discouraging Henry, might well add lustre to his other desirable qualities, for Henry VIII was so enamored of gentle blood that he occasionally ennobled an intimate if he lacked that quality.

On the other hand, his age was a serious drawback, and there is more truth than poetry in Shakespeare's lines that:

> Crabbed age and youth cannot live together:
> Youth is full of pleasance, age is full of care;
> Youth like summer morn, age like winter weather;
> Youth like summer brave, age like winter bare.
> Youth is full of sport, age's breath is short;
> Youth is nimble, age is lame;
> Youth is hot and bold, age is weak and cold;
> Youth is wild, and age is tame.[39]

Brittle bones and tired muscles ruled out participation in such physically demanding sports as jousting, wrestling, and fighting at the barriers. Though the earl could not enjoy these warlike games with

[39]   Shakespeare, p. 1405.

his sovereign, he was fortunate in having a son and son-in-law who could. The king numbered among his active companions, Surrey's second son, Edward, and his son-in-law, Sir Thomas Knyvett. Edward Howard, the Lord Admiral, became one of the heroic figures of his age: his daring feats as a sea captain who raided the French towns along the French coast, swept the French fleet from the English Channel, and captured the ships of Andrew Barton, the famous Scottish pirate, made Edward a living legend when he died at the age of thirty-six in a foolhardy attempt to board a French vessel. Only a little less illustrious than his brother-in-law was Sir Thomas Knyvett, the king's standard bearer and the Master of Horse, who married Edward's sister Muriel Howard, the widow of John Grey, viscount Lisle. Knyvett was just as brave and rash as the admiral, and he too died a hero's death in a naval engagement against the French.[40] Both men were bosom companions to the king. Whenever the king jousted or held a special entertainment, both men were likely to be fighting or frolicking at the king's side. For example, Edward fought at the barriers with Henry on May 23, 27, and June 1, 1510, and Knyvett celebrated the arrival of a royal male heir by taking part in jousts which Henry arranged in honor of the occasion. Knyvett was with Henry when the king, at a royal pageant, was discovered by the people of London who joyfully stripped their monarch and his companion to their hose.[41] The love that the king held for his comrades-in-arms was a love almost surpassing man's love for woman, like that of the fabled Roland for his friend Oliver.

Could Surrey take advantage of the king's affection for his kin and turn it to political advantage? This was a crucial question for Surrey and his faction. Its answer depended on several variables: the earl's ability to manipulate his relatives, their talent for influencing the king, the tractability of the king, the political maneuvers of other councillors, and that great arbiter of many men's fortunes — chance. At the time of Henry VII's death, two councillors, Surrey and Fox, had the greatest opportunity of exercising supreme control in the council. Three months after the old king's death, Margaret Beaufort, Henry VIII's grandmother, thought by many to have great influence with the young king, died and left the field open to these two. They did not have to worry about Wolsey, since he was not yet sworn of the

---

[40] *Memorials*, Appendix V; *L. P.*, I, 120, 369.
[41] *L. P.*, I, 1491, Appendix no. 9; Edward Hall, *Henry VIII*, ed. by Charles Whibley, 2 vols. (London, 1904), I, 22-27.

council and did not become a councillor until November.[42] They busily began to align the different councillors into two opposing camps. Pollard has theorized that the party which clung to Surrey was "... warlike, feudal, anti-clerical, or merely factious ...", but the matter, as Pollard notes, is not quite that simple, since Surrey opposed initiating a French war in 1512.[43] Surrey's supporters in August 1509 included George Talbot, the earl of Shrewsbury; Thomas Ruthal, the bishop of Durham; Sir Henry Marney; Charles Brandon; and Thomas, lord Darcy. Talbot was one of Surrey's associates in the exchequer since he was Chamberlain of the Exchequer. Marny was captain of the King's Guard and Chancellor of the Duchy of Lancaster. Brandon was an intimate of both Knyvett and Edward Howard and also one of the convivial comrades of the young king. Ruthal was then secretary to the king and an opportunist willing to attach himself to whomever he thought would be on the winning side. Darcy was Treasurer of Berwick and Warden of the East March, and in a manner of speaking, one of Surrey's successors in the North. Although Surrey was the chief man in his faction, his enlistment of the Chancellor, Archbishop Warham, to his side[44] may indicate that he felt neither able nor energetic enough to rule by himself.

Apparently the balance between the two factions was very delicate, for there was a rumor current that Fox hoped to rule all by securing the aid of the Duke of Buckingham, whose daughter married Surrey's son Thomas in 1512, and of the Earl of Northumberland.[45] As the factional struggle developed, its outcome turned on two points: the king's personality and foreign diplomacy. Whoever had the king's ear could control the situation. Since the king had expensive tastes, such as rich apparel, fine cuisine, and the maintenance of a vast number of personal retainers all gorgeously attired, some historians have thought Surrey used his office as treasurer to manipulate the purse strings to play a tune pleasing to Henry VIII. These historians have indicted him as being the one responsible for the dissipation of Henry VII's treasure. Even so modern a historian as James D. Mackie does not scruple to point a finger of shame at the treasurer for using his position "... to promote a lavish expenditure ...".[46] Mackie is

---

[42] Polydore Vergil, pp. 152, 194; *Wolsey*, p. 13.
[43] *Ibid.*, p. 11.
[44] *L. P.*, I, 25, 27, 71, 75, 391. See also *L. P.*, "Preface", I, xiii.
[45] *Ibid.*, 157.
[46] Mackie, p. 233.

careful to point out that these new expenditures do not appear in the chamber accounts, but that wages of musicians, falconers, and minstrels tended to go up.[47] And a not so recent historian, Patrick F. Tytler, in his *Life of Henry VIII* recounts Surrey's steady and faithful employment under Henry VII and then theorizes that the earl's character underwent a Jekyl-Hyde transformation on the accession of Henry VIII, that the earl studied the new king's character to the intent of improving his own fortune by feeding the king's appetite for pageant and spectacle. Another author repeats the tale that Surrey got the king involved in pursuit of his pleasures so that the king's ministers could manage state affairs, while still another says that it was not Surrey but Wolsey who encouraged this spendthrift policy and that the earl pursued a moderate path between the extremes of the penny-pinching Fox and the expenditure-minded Wolsey.[48] Wherein lies the truth? Who was responsible for the increased expenditures?

It seems incorrect to assume, as did Tytler, that Surrey's character underwent a startling metamorphosis at Henry VIII's accession. The earl did not change colors like a chameleon. He did adjust to the personality of the new king, but this had always been his métier — his ability to present a favorable image of himself to his king. It is nonsense to say that he became a different person with the arrival of Henry VIII on the scene: he was the same person operating on the same principle as before — what will please the king, how can I gain his favor? With Henry VII favor was obtained by Spartan self-discipline and in the performance of arduous administrative, financial, diplomatic, and conciliar duties. With Henry VIII there was an emphasis on looking-up, laughing, and living — letting the heart delight in a magnificent court. A courtier would have to have been myopic indeed not to have perceived this fundamental difference in attitude between the old king, whose precarious youth accustomed him to a spare existence, and the new king brought up as heir to the throne and determined as a result of his upbringing to enjoy the fruits of kingship.

Where the old king accounted for every farthing, the new king let pounds slip through his fingers like quicksilver. For example, Henry VII had fined the Earl of Northumberland £10,000 for abducting

[47] *Ibid.*
[48] Patrick Fraser Tytler, *Life Of King Henry The Eighth*, 2nd ed. (Edinburgh, 1837), pp. 19-20; Dallaway, II, pt. 1, 198; Gerald Brenan and Edward Phillips Statham, *The House Of Howard*, 2 vols. (New York, 1908), I, 81.

Elizabeth Hastyngs, the daughter and heiress of Sir John Hastyngs, and Henry VIII pardoned him from the payment of his fine.[49] Henry was forever forgiving his nobles for nonpayment of debts to the crown. Even Wolsey complained of the king's extravagances; he was especially piqued when in 1511 the king forgave Thomas, lord Darcy, of a loan of £1000.[50] Fundamentally then, the answer to responsibility for new expenditures is inherent in the new king's character. He liked lavish display more than his father. He was a young king who delighted in the tremendous resources at his disposal. If he wanted magnificent court spectacles that were expensive, why should he not have them — he was king, was he not?

Let this fledgling king learn the true extent of his powers and his advisors would not be able to direct his flights of fancy. He was more than a majestic eagle which needs its daily ration of game and exercise. Behind the sharp eye and bright plumage lurked a political intelligence of the first order. The attraction of the hunt, the delight in court pageantry might dazzle and benumb this intelligence for a time, but frequent forays into the field of international diplomacy taught valuable lessons which were not easily forgotten. For a time, jousting, love-making, and play acting appeared to have won the day. But appearances can be deceiving, especially in an era when most government was conducted on a personal level. The king could run the government of England almost as well when he was hawking with the members of his court, who made up the inner ring of councillors, as when he was in his council chamber. That he took the time for fighting at the barriers, wrestling, and sports of the field does not necessarily mean he neglected his government. As he wrote to his father-in-law, King Ferdinand, during the summer of 1509: He was diverting "... himself with jousts, birding, hunting, and other innocent and honest pastimes, also in visiting part of his kingdom . . .", but he was not on that account neglecting "affairs of state".[51]

Henry's casual comment about his activities indicates the relaxed approach he took to both his pleasures and his politics. Far from indicating a basic lack of concern or lack of understanding of state affairs, it points to his awareness of his responsibility in and to his government. All sovereignty ultimately resided in him; the state could

[49] L. P., I, 414 (58).
[50] P. S. and H. M. Allen (eds.), Letters Of Richard Fox 1486-1527 (Oxford, 1929), p. 54.
[51] C. S. P. Span., II, 19.

not be separated from the person of the king. As he told the House of Commons in 1543: "We be informed by our Judges that we at no time stand so high in our estate royal as in the time of Parliament, when we as head and you as members are conjoined and knit together in one body politic."[52] He did think in constructive terms about kingship, and realized instinctively that his advisors and even the parliamentarians were only associated in government through his person. Almost from the start of his reign, Henry divined the nature of his authority. The careers of Wolsey and Thomas Cromwell have often been cited as examples of Henry's failure to manage English politics, but both men ultimately fell from power as a result of the king's disfavor. For a while, Henry might allow an *alter rex* to exist in the person of a servile minister, but only for a while. The real master of the situation was the king.

But the king needed useful, able, energetic servants. Were either Fox or Surrey exactly the type of deputy he required? The handling of his diplomacy would tell whether one of the two or another would meet his requirements. When Henry ascended the throne, the Venetian ambassador ascertained that the young king was hostile to France. His hostility became quite evident in August when he flew into a towering rage because someone had written a conciliatory dispatch to France. There are grounds for believing that Surrey or someone in his faction was responsible for writing it, and this view is consistent with Surrey's anti-war policy of 1512. As a consequence of this letter, the king thought that only Fox was fit for handling French diplomacy, since he believed that many of the other councillors were pensioners of the French king. And Fox's following of the king's lead may have been the reason for his temporary ascendancy in the council in 1510, for the Venetian ambassador spoke of him as *alter rex*. But Fox's ascendancy was short-lived; he became ill, which not only prevented Andrea Badoer, the Venetian ambassador, from obtaining copies of Henry's correspondence from Fox,[53] but also probably gave Wolsey his opportunity.

Thomas Wolsey, the king's almoner, by dint of hard work, diligence, and a brilliant flair for mastering detail was slowly working his way into the king's confidence. He was brought into the council in November 1509 and according to Polydore Vergil, he owed his place to

---

[52] Quoted in G. M. Trevelyan, *History Of England*, 3rd ed., 3 vols. (London, 1952), II, 58.
[53] *L. P.*, I, 156, 430, 434, 476.

Fox's desire to use his talents against Surrey. One of the signs of Henry's favor was Wolsey's election in 1510 as registrar to the order of the garter.[54] The almoner was soon thinking of ways in which he could supplant both Surrey and Fox in the council chamber and in the affections of his king. One way was to urge Henry to make war on France which would mean upsetting the old king's practice of peace with all foreign countries and would also mean antagonizing a considerable number of Henry VIII's councillors. The policy was a dangerous one since a new Anglo-French peace treaty had been negotiated in March 1510 by Surrey, Fox, and Ruthal,[55] and the principal architects of the treaty would no doubt defend it as good statesmanship. But Wolsey assessed the new king's character carefully, and he realized that Henry would enthusiastically accept any excuse for war. A war policy was consistent with Henry's desire for foreign conquest and his chivalric orientation. He wished for only the opportunity to test his prowess in real battle and to prove to himself that he was a *prud homme* and *le bon chevalier*.

The decision to fight France came late in 1511 and may very well have been a cause of Surrey's leaving the court in disgrace. Writing to Bishop Fox on September 30, 1511, Wolsey gleefully reported that a week ago the king showed such displeasure at Surrey's appearance that the earl had departed, and in a not less charitable vein he added that: "With lytyll help nowe he myght be vtterly, as towchyng loggyng in the same, [court] excludyd: wherof in my poore iuggement no lytyll goode shuld insue."[56] If the king wished to initiate a war with France and Surrey opposed him, his dismissal is understandable. Of course, a possible alternative to war with France was war with Scotland, a project vigorously supported by Surrey's son Edward. But war with Scotland did not seem to Henry to hold the potential triumps of a Henry V over France. Wolsey was especially concerned that Edward Howard "... meruelusly incendyth the Kyng ayenst the Scottis: by whos wantone meanys hys grace spendyth / mych money, and ys more dyssposyd to ware than paxe. Yowr presence / shalbe very necessary to represse thys appetyte."[57] Wolsey wanted war, but he wanted it to be his war and not a fabrication of the Howard family. He wanted to make sure that he was in charge.

[54] Polydore Vergil, p. 194; *L. P.*, I, 442.
[55] *C. S. P. Span.*, II, 36.
[56] *Letters of Fox*, p. 54.
[57] *Ibid.*

Wolsey was playing a dangerous game by staking his reputation on the success or failure of a very hazardous foreign enterprise. Rumors were rife on the continent that the great men of England thought he was the author of the French war and would hold him accountable for its failure. William Knight, the diplomatic agent in Spain, repeated the rumors and implored him to be cautious.[58] But Wolsey threw caution to the winds, he risked everything because he was confident of his ability to manage affairs and, perhaps, even the king. As long as the king was behind him, he knew he need fear no one — neither Surrey nor his superior Fox. With impunity, Wolsey broke Fox's instructions while the latter was ill and did not deliver to the king Fox's recommendations for a new pope. Instead, Wolsey substituted his own.[59] Although he begged Fox to hurry back to court to help him reduce the Howard influence, the almoner may just as well have hoped to benefit from the possibility of Fox being discountenanced at court. If both Surrey and Fox were turned out, then Wolsey might be even more certain of the young king's favor.

Henry did not heed the advice of his old councillors, but made definite plans to fight France and placed Wolsey in charge of the operation. By a treaty which Surrey and the Earl of Shrewsbury negotiated with Spain in November 1511, England and Spain became military allies. Under the terms of the treaty, England was to attack France by April 30, 1512 and each side agreed to make no separate peace. While Ferdinand, the king of Spain, pursued a policy of smoke-and-glory in Italy, Henry was to create a second front in France against their mutual enemy.[60] The idea was much to Henry's liking. At last he would have an opportunity to emulate the heroes he imitated in his court revels, and he would be trying to reassert the dominance of English arms in France, a traditionally popular policy with the English people. Not only was this policy in keeping with the English king's chivalric interests, but it may have been inspired in part by Henry's wife, Catherine of Aragon, Ferdinand's daughter. When Henry first married her, he genuinely cared for her and was anxious to please her. He thought of her more as the romantic heroine of the chivalric tales he fed on, than as a mere wife. Eleven days after his coronation he wrote to Ferdinand: "The bond between them is now so strict that all their interests are common, and the love he

[58] *L. P.*, I, 1422.
[59] *Letters of Fox*, pp. 52-53.
[60] *C. S. P. Span.*, II, 59; *L. P.*, I, 969 (29).

bears to Catherine is such, that if he were still free he would choose her in preference to all others."[61] Henry's war policy was probably urged on him by Catherine who was acting in her father's interest.[62] Who can blame Ferdinand for taking advantage of Henry who guilelessly told his father-in-law all the secrets locked in his heart? Henry soon learned by bitter experience, that trust put in kings is often misplaced.

While the lot of managing the French enterprise fell to Wolsey and not to Surrey, nevertheless, he and his sons figured actively in the king's plans for the coming struggle. Surrey's son, Edward, fresh from his victory over the Scottish pirate, Andrew Barton, was entrusted with the command of England's navy. The old earl derived huge satisfaction from the fact "... that while he had an estate that could furnish a ship, or son capable of commanding one, the narrow seas should not be infested".[63] And now his second born son was in charge of the king's military forces by sea; Edward Howard was made Admiral and commander-in-chief of the fleet on April 7, 1512 and he waited during that month at Plymouth Road, momentarily expecting an engagement with the French. Edward's elder brother, Thomas, found a place in the military forces of the Marquis of Dorset and was commissioned to be Dorset's successor as Lieutenant-General of the army should the Marquis be killed or incapacitated in battle. Their father was left to protect the northern frontier against the Scots, the traditional allies of the French. In April, Surrey took musters at Greenwich; on July 31 he received a commission of array for Yorkshire, Northumberland, Cumberland, Westmoreland, and Lancashire; and on August 1 he accepted the banner of the cross of St. George and the Red Dragon standard and went to Yorkshire to levy soldiers. After ascertaining that all was quiet, he returned to London. There was peace with Scotland, a peace which one author says Fox urged on Henry in opposition to the wishes of Surrey and his son Thomas.[64]

War with Scotland was much to be preferred to war with France, for in fighting Scotland there was little possibility that France, deeply

---

[61]   *Ibid.*, 119.
[62]   On July 29, 1509 Catherine wrote to her father telling him that she had acted as his ambassador. *Ibid.*, 127.
[63]   *Memorials*, Appendix V.
[64]   *Ibid.*; L. P., I, 1170 (7), 1221 (48), 1317, 1365 (3), 1748; Edmund C. Batten, ed., *The Register Of Richard Fox, While Bishop Of Bath And Wells. A. D. MCCCCXCII-MCCCCXCIV* (London, 1889), p. 90.

committed to European military adventures, would give much aid and comfort to Scotland. On the other hand, a French war, which would engage the best English soldiers and sailors, and would leave the English realm with a skeleton defense force at best, would make Scottish invasion an attractive and practicable policy to James IV. If war were limited to Scotland, the Howards might exert a powerful influence over the mind of Henry. Edward was thoroughly familiar with the North country, where he grew up and had won his spurs. His father knew the intricacies of northern defence and the niceties of launching border raids into the Scottish Marches. Of all the nobles in the kingdom, the aging earl had spent more time in battle than any.

His presence on a northern campaign would be invaluable and almost indispensable to his king. If, however, the king was determined to make war on France, he would have to protect himself against Scotland and at least leave a force strong enough to repel the Scots. And if by some chance the earl should be left behind to defend the realm against Scotland, he was faced with the sickening prospect of losing personal contact with the king — while Wolsey took advantage of the situation.

The complexity of the situation did not escape Surrey. As with other nobles, he suffered from the misfortune of being an especially useful military instrument. His bravery and military prowess removed him from the circle of active councillors precisely when he most needed to be at the king's side. Instead of being with the king, he was off during a great part of 1512 seeing to the defense of the North, and at the same time his sons Thomas and Edward and his son-in-law Knyvett were on naval and military duty which also removed them from the king's side. But this was not the only misfortune which Surrey was to suffer in 1512 and 1513. The very bravery which recommended Edward and Knyvett to the king as his special boon companions cost them their lives. Misfortune was piled atop misfortune. On August 12, 1512 Knyvett went to the rescue of Charles Brandon's ship, the *Sovereign*, which had attacked the French ship, the *Cordelier*. Knyvett came in for some close fighting with the French ship, grappled with her, and then he and his men burned to death as a fire suddenly spread from one ship to the other. Edward was thunderstruck and felt in some way as if his brother-in-law's death were his fault. He vowed never to look the king in the face until he had avenged Knyvett's death. Touched to the quick by this unfortunate incident and the death of his sister, Knyvett's widow,[65] who did not long survive her husband, the admiral soon proved the truth of his maxim that "... Never did sea-man good that was not resolute to a degree of madnesse."[66] He sought out the French continually and lost his life on April 25, 1513 in a foolish attempt to board a French vessel. His boarding party was overpowered and in the melee the admiral was pushed overboard into the sea where he drowned.[67]

His loss to the Howard family was irreparable, for though Surrey had two full grown sons, Thomas and Edmund, neither was the equal of Edward. Thomas was a decent enough soldier and sailor and competently filled in as Lord Admiral for his brother, but he did not have the élan which Edward possessed. He got along well with Henry, but he never captured and commanded his sovereign's heart in the way in which an Edward or Thomas Knyvett could. Thomas was, if anything, even more violent than his father and less intelligent since he had more pride and made little attempt to conceal it. In his hour of triumph when Wolsey fell in 1529, he proved unequal to the task of managing England's affairs. In short, he was a fit servant, but a poor manager. As for Edmund, he never got close enough to Henry VIII to win his favor: for some reason Henry did not seem to like Edmund and consequently he never achieved high office.[68] Thus, the loss of Surrey's sons materially reduced the possibility of his influence with the king at a time when he most needed them in his fight with Wolsey, the new manager of the French war.

An English invasion of France was imminent. The final Anglo-Spanish alliance for the conduct of the war was concluded on April 18, 1513, specifying that England should declare war on France within thirty days.[69] War became a certainty. Amidst the bustle and excitement of making preparations for the coming expedition there was much talk among the councillors as to who should go with Henry and who should stay behind. Someone had to stay. Catherine could

---

[65] *Memorials*, Appendix V; *L. P.*, "Preface", I, xvi. Surrey's army was paid for eighty-four days from August 4 to October 27, 1512 with the earl receiving £5 per day. *Ibid.*, 1450. For the wills of Edward Howard and Muriel Knyvett see *Test. Vet.*, II, 516, 533-34.

[66] B. M. Sloane 1523, fol. 33 (r).

[67] *Memorials*, Appendix V.

[68] For a discussion of Edmund Howard's unfortunate career see Lacey Baldwin Smith, *A Tudor Tragedy: The Life and Times of Catherine Howard* (London, 1961), pp. 38-44.

[69] *C. S. P. Span.*, II, 99, 100, 101.

not be expected to manage affairs of state without the help of proven councillors and a military force sufficient to repel the Scots should they attack. Not a councillor wished to remain. Obviously to be out of the king's sight was to be out of mind: favor followed the person of the king. In the past year the Howards had been away from Henry and his court: Lord Thomas and Edward on naval expeditions and Surrey in the North seeing to its defence. To be away from the king too frequently would mean the loss or diminution of their influence with him. It was imperative to Surrey that he accompany the king to France if he wished to dominate the council and prevent Wolsey from becoming the king's first minister. For Surrey, the question of whether or not he would be allowed to go to France was far more than a quest for glory, it was a matter of practical politics upon which he rested all the hopes of his house.

These hopes were doomed to disappointment; he was not to go. Instead, he remained in England as one of Catherine's council and as a bulwark against the Scottish threat. Was Surrey's disappointment a result of Wolsey's clever maneuvering or was it the result of independent action on the part of Henry? Probably a little bit of both. Why should Henry want this old campaigner at his elbow at every turn telling him what to do and reminding him how it was done at Barnet, Bosworth, and Ackworth. The king wanted to enjoy himself; he wished to savour this campaign to the fullest. Besides, England could not be left unguarded and there should be honor enough for this old man in serving the king's queen. The duty was not unimportant, it was a position of trust given only to one who held the king's supreme confidence. On leaving England, Henry took Surrey by the hand and said: "My lord, I trust not the Scotts; therefore I pray you be not negligent."[70] As Henry embarked for Calais on June 30, 1513, he left the old earl standing on the English shore, as Garrett Mattingly says "... choking with rage and grief at missing the triumphs in France...".[71] Little did Surrey know that he would win such a triumph at Flodden that the king's feats at Tournai would seem pale in comparison.

---

[70] Ellis, *Letters*, I, 86.
[71] Mattingly, *Catherine Of Aragon*, p. 71.

V

FLODDEN

It is one of the great ironies of history that Henry VIII's successful campaign of the Summer and Fall of 1513 should be obscured by Surrey's success on Flodden Field. While his king was methodically battering down the walls of French armed cities and achieving great military triumphs at Terouenne and Tournai, the septuagenarian earl hastily mustered his men, took the field, forced a fight with James IV, and won a smashing victory despite the fact that his troops fought with parched lips and empty stomachs. The circumstances surrounding his victory and the strategy used by the crafty earl caught the imagination of his contemporaries as had those of no other battle, for they saw in them Divine Providence at work. For ever afterwards the Scots would look to Flodden as a national disaster, but the English would hail it as a national deliverance. Like Gideon, who routed tens of thousands of Midianites with three hundred men armed only with lamps, pitchers, and swords, Surrey conquered a force numerically superior to his own. His achievement, in view of the rumours that James IV's forces numbered 100,000 compared to the earl's 26,000,[1] seemed so stupendous that only the miraculous could explain it: hence the common acceptance of the idea that ". . . God gave the stroke . . .".[2] How else could an army outnumbered four to one have defeated a vastly superior enemy? As always, the superstitious found a ready answer: God fought for our side.

Surrey won, according to his contemporaries, not because he was a better general than James, but because God fought for him and directed his strategy. It is only fitting, then, that the most famous portrait of Surrey should show him in coat of mail and surcoat praying

---

[1] William Garret (ed.), *The Battle Of Flodden Field* (Newcastle, 1822). The original manuscript for this edition was printed by Richard Fawkes in 1535 and is usually referred to as the *Trewe Encountre*.

[2] Hall, p. 109.

Fig. 2. Thomas Howard, Earl of Surrey on the morning of Flodden

before the battle of Flodden. Above all, the portrait seems to say that the earl was about to win because he was a virtuous man fighting against a treacherous king who had falsely broken the Anglo-Scottish peace treaty. In a certain sense it is just to remember Surrey principally for his part at Flodden, for it was one of the key events in his life; but it is unjust to think of him, as do many historians, only in connection with Flodden, for he also had a distinguished career as one of Henry VIII's councillors. One must also remember that there is another portrait of Surrey which depicts him in councillor's garb.[3] Be that as it may, Surrey did have a good deal to do with Flodden and by today's historical standards he was much more than God's instrument.

His stubborn, human pride had as much to do with his attitude toward the Scots as his faith in God. When he had taken his leave of Henry at Dover, he was so overcome by emotion that he was speechless with rage and vexation. Once he had gained control of himself, he made a vow that if he ever got the chance, he would make the Scottish king sorry that he had been the cause of his remaining in England.[4] If he wanted God's help, it was only to vindicate his pride and to wreak his vengeance on James. Surrey could not let James devastate the England which Henry had entrusted to him, nor would he allow himself to think of defeat. He knew he could not fail, for his professional reputation as a soldier and his personal honor were at stake. Though he was desperate, he was also confident, for he knew his enemy intimately, both as a former adversary in the 1490's and as a friend in 1503. As a tennis player who is playing an opponent whom he has beaten many times, he thought himself to be complete master of the situation.

The English had need of all the dedication and devotion to God and country which they could muster in the face of James IV's projected invasion. Again, popular imagination saw Surrey's soldiers in the role of their country's deliverers, much as the soldiers of Joan of Arc must have appeared to the fifteenth century French. Even the Venetian, Nicolo DiFavri, noted the disparity between the Italian mercenaries who would rather pillage than fight and Surrey's men who sought honor at their own cost. The English soldiers single-mindedness of purpose was evident in his abstinence from swearing

---

3 See Figures 2 and 3, facing p. 105 and 109 respectively.
4 Hall, p. 96.

and wenching and his reliance on prayer for spiritual sustenance.[5]
Like a mighty army engaged in a holy crusade, the English soldiers
marched north to defend their country from the barbarous onslaught
of the perfidious Scots.

If God were fighting for the English, than He obviously was against
the Scots. But the matter was not that simple, for both Henry and
James were Christian princes, each highly religious. Just prior to
invading England, James IV, an inveterate pilgrim, paid a call at the
shrine of St. Duthac. Perhaps, then, the saints like the gods and
goddesses in Homeric epics were taking individual sides: St. Duthac
for the Scots and St. George and St. Cuthbert for the English.[6] Both
sides were convinced of the essential rightness of its position. James IV
had a long list of grievances which he catalogued as he prepared for
war; the English had slain the great Scottish sea captain, Andrew
Barton, without provocation; the English were molesting the French
Duke of Gueldres, a personal friend of James's; the English had
caused the French king to lose Milan and were now invading France
without good reason; the English ambassador at Rome, Christopher
Bainbridge, the archbishop of York, was turning the Pope against
James; the English denied safe conduct to the Scottish agents of
James; the English without regard for justice gave asylum to the
Bastard Heron, who had willfully murdered Sir Robert Ker, Warden
of the Scottish Middle March; and finally and most grievously, the
English king persisted in withholding Henry VII's legacy from James's
wife Margaret.[7]

The English were quite willing to let James have his wife's legacy
for a price, and that price was James's promise that he would not
attack England during Henry's absence. The painstaking diplomacy
of Henry's special envoy to Scotland, Dr. Nicholas West, was directed
towards securing Scotland's neutrality. But Dr. West was fishing in
troubled waters. To all his demands and requests for assurance that
James would not go to war, James, at first, gave evasive answers.
When West offered Margaret's legacy, James refused, telling the
Englishman he preferred his French alliance to that of Henry, and he
would not send an ambassador to England because he feared that such

[5]   C. S. P. Ven., I, 333.
[6]   R. L. Mackie, King James IV Of Scotland: A Brief Survey of His Life and
Times (London, 1958), p. 244; Hall, p. 99.
[7]   L. P., I, 2122. G. Gregory Smith (ed.), The Days Of James IIII, 1488-1513
(London, 1900), p. 144.

action would lose him the French king. The real reason for James's policy became apparent in May of 1513 when he pleaded with Henry to renounce his foolish policy of French conquest and unite with him in a Holy Crusade versus the Turkish infidels.[8] Clinging to the medieval ideal of the unity of Christendom, the Scottish king hoped to conciliate the major European powers and to concentrate their military resources in a holy assault on the rapidly growing Turkish empire. Of course, in so doing, he would win renown both as a general and as a true son of the church.

The Holy League entered into by the Pope, the Emperor, Ferdinand, and Henry distressed him. By its terms, the Pope was to invade Provence or Dauphiny, the Emperor to invade any part of France he desired, Henry to attack the French in Picardy, Aquitaine, or Normandy, and Ferdinand to launch an offensive in Bearne, Languedoc, or Aquitaine. Though the Holy League was not concluded until April 5, 1513, James had knowledge that on April 1 Ferdinand had signed a truce with Louis XII. Since James wished to prevent a general war at any cost, he sent news of the truce and a plea for peace to Henry.[9] Henry would have none of it; he had made up his mind on war and to war he would go. Neither could he believe that that master of duplicity, Ferdinand, would have the temerity to double-cross his son-in-law. Such is the naivety of headstrong youth.

Besides, Henry's intelligence from Dacre and Fox indicated that the Scots were not likely to fight. The current rumour on the continent was that there would be no Anglo-Scottish war. Fox saw little possibility of Anglo-Scottish land engagements, but he did think the Scots might attack and rob English ships. As late as June 25, Dacre, the warden or the marches, reported that there was no likelihood of war. Thus, Henry's mind was at ease as he sailed for France accompanied by his principal advisors, such as Bishop Fox, who had one hundred and two retainers in his personal retinue, and Thomas Wolsey, the king's unofficial war minister, who brought two hundred and fifty-eight personal retainers.[10] The ascendancy of the almoner over the king was nearly complete, and success in the French enterprise would raise his stock considerably.

When James's representative, Lyon Herald, appeared on French soil before Henry on August thirteenth to announce the Scottish

[8] *L. P.*, I, 1735, 1922.
[9] *Ibid.*, 1750, 1922.
[10] *Ibid.*, 1960, 2014, 2026, 2053.

king's declaration of war, Henry was not so much surprised as vexed. He peevishly inquired of Lyon Herald what his brother-in-law wanted of him. The herald replied that his presence was required in England, and it was James's wish that Henry should return at once to his realm. Henry haughtily told the Scotsman that he would return when he pleased and not at James's command. Henry was not going to give up his chance at achieving fame in France because of a little trouble engineered by James. Let James attack if he must. Let him do his worst, for the king had left his kingdom well provided. Had he not "...left an erle [Surrey] in my realme at home which shalbe able to defende him and all his powre...".[11] Henry probably did not expect James to fight, and he suspected him of dreaming up this threat of war to dissuade him from his French adventures. If the Scottish king were successful in calling a halt to Henry's French campaign, his vision of a universal crusade against the Turk was one step closer to reality.

But James was not merely making war with words. He intended to carry out his threat, for at the same time that Lyon Herald was speaking with Henry, Alexander, Lord Hume, the warden of the Scottish eastern march, was laying waste to the English countryside. Fortunately for the English, Hume and his men were intercepted and badly beaten by Sir William Bulmer, the English warden of the East March, before they could return to Scotland Scot-free.[12] James, himself, left Edinburgh on August nineteenth, two days after his artillery. He crossed the Tweed River into England on the twenty-second and invested Norham castle whch fell after a six day siege. He spent the remainder of the month in battering down any English castle which chanced to be in his path and was comfortably situated at Castle Ford on September fourth. His leisurely pace in campaigning — he had only gone six miles into England in two weeks — may be attributed to his general strategy of forcing Henry to come home, rather than that of initiating a general war, though some say James's military progress was slowed down considerably by his introduction to the mistress of Ford Castle.[13]

[11] Hall, p. 76.
[12] *Ibid.*, p. 97; Gerald F. T. Leather, *New Light On Flodden*, 2nd ed. (Berwick, 1938), p. 76.
[13] R. L. Mackie, p. 249. Origin of the tale of James's adultery with Lady Heron is usually traced to Pittscottie's Chronicle. Robert Lindesay of Pitscottie, *The Historie and Cronicles of Scotland*, ed. by A. E. J. G. MacKay, 3 vols. (Edinburgh-London, 1899-1911), I, 262-4.

Fig. 3. Thomas Howard, Duke of Norfolk

Lady Heron, the fascinating lady in question, has even been made the heroine of a romantic poem in which she betrays James for the love of her "Martial voluptuary" Surrey. Surrey is portrayed more as a virile Hotspur than as a tired, seventy year old general. Of course, the poem has a tragic, but moral ending: the honorable Surrey rejects Lady Heron who remorsefully stabs herself when she realizes her treachery has caused James's death.[14] The poem has little foundation in historical fact, and the most recent biographer of James, Mr. R. L. Mackie, rejects the old legend that James lost valuable time in dallying with Lady Heron.[15]

While James contented himself with the capture of a few English castles and awaited the appearance of an English force, his antagonist, Surrey, was extremely busy. As soon as he was apprized of Scottish intentions, he left for the North on July twenty-second and arrived at Pontefract castle on the first of the following month. The month of August was spent in making preparations for the coming campaign. On August twenty-fifth, he requested all able-bodied men to meet with him at Newcastle on September first. He then started north to keep the appointed rendezvous in the foulest weather imaginable. At one river crossing the waves beat so high and were so strong that his guide nearly drowned, ". . . yet he never ceased, but kept on hys jorney to geve example to them that shoulde folowe".[16] As Surrey went about the business of putting an army in the field, Catherine, the queen, fidgeted at her palace, raised a standby reserve army, and worried about her husband who had just won the Battle of Spurs. She was quite light-hearted about the prospect of fighting the Scots and boastfully wrote to Wolsey that as far as war was concerned: "My heart is very good to it, and I am horribly busy with making (of) standards, banners, and badges."[17] As if her banners and badges would win the battle, and not her loyal subjects. But her faith in banners, especially those which displayed religious emblems, was also shared by Thomas Ruthal who later attributed Surrey's victory to the intercession of St. Cuthbert under whose banner the earl fought.[18]

Surrey reached Alnwich on September third and joyfully welcomed his son Thomas, the Lord Admiral, and one thousand stout-hearted

---

[14] Alfred Austin, *Flodden Field: A Tragedy* (New York, 1903).
[15] R. D. Mackie, pp. 249-50.
[16] Hall, p. 99.
[17] *L. P.*, I, 2162.
[18] *Ibid.*, 2283.

Englishmen on the following day. With the appearance of his son, Surrey's forces were complete, numbering roughly twenty thousand men which was a slightly smaller force that that of the Scots. The figures estimating the Scottish force at either 100,000 men or 80,000 men, though contemporary, are greatly exaggerated. Even Bishop Ruthal reported to Wolsey that James had lost at least 20,000 men by desertion since the siege of Norham.[19] Almost from the beginning of his campaign, James was faced with the difficult task of keeping his men from slipping away. Many left as soon as they had their fill of looting, and the attitude of most seems to have been that their object was to produce a gigantic raid on the English and not to fight a pitched battle.

With the Lord Admiral in the English camp, battle assignments were given to the various captains. Surrey's son Thomas was given the coveted post of commanding the army's van and the commanders of his wings were Edmund Howard on the right and Marmaduke Constable on the left. The earl, himself, took charge of the rear and appointed Lord Dacre commander of his right wing and Sir Edward Stanley commander of the left wing. At an evening parley it was decided to send the herald, Rouge Croix, with an offer of battle to James. Rouge Croix was instructed to tell the king that the English would release their Scottish prisoners, George Hume and Lord Johnstone, if he would promise not to destroy Ford castle. Lord Thomas Howard added a personal message to the official communication: inform the Scottish king of my presence in my father's camp and let him do what he will about his revenge, for I am ready and waiting for him.[20] Lord Thomas's challenge was more than an empty boast, for there was method as well as good will couched in it. He hoped to goad James into an immediate engagement which the English considered necessary in view of their perilous position. They were getting dangerously low on supplies, for in two days they would be out of beer and in four, food itself. If Surrey were to keep his army in the field, he had to fight soon; and the sooner the better.

On the fifth, the earl removed to Bolton in Glendale where he mustered his men. Meanwhile, James detained Rouge Croix, possibly because he did not wish the herald to bring the English news of his

[19] Hall, pp. 99-100; *Trewe Encountre*; *L. P.*, I, 2246, 2283; R. L. Mackie, pp. 251-52.
[20] Hall, pp. 100-02. *D. N. B.*, article on Alexander Home. Apparently no deal was made, for James burned Ford Castle before moving on to Flodden Edge. R. L. Mackie, p. 254.

forces or of his new position at Flodden Edge, and on the next day he sent his own herald, Ilay, to accept the English offer of battle which was set for Friday, the ninth. Surrey met James's herald and requested that sureties to the amount of £10,000 be entered into to insure that a battle take place.[21]

The earl's eagerness to fight was, of course, inspired by his knowledge that his supplies were running low. He hoped by appealing to James's sense of honor and regard for ancient chivalric custom, to make doubly sure that his elusive opponent would fight. Though the Scottish king seemed to have taken the bait, there was little cause for elation as Surrey was to discover when he moved his army to Wooler. There it was possible for the English to view the Scots, firmly entrenched at Flodden Edge, a scant three miles from Wooler. James had an almost impregnable position on top of one of the Cheviot hills, which was protected on one side by a large marsh, on another by the Cheviot hills, and by ordinance in the front. To have attacked James where he stood would have been folly, and Surrey knew it. Therefore, he sent Rouge Croix, who had since returned, to James with a request that the king descend the hill and fight in the open. James knew his advantage and would not budge. He scornfully rejected the earl's demand that the Scots fight the English on the flat Milfield Plain,[22] and he denied that he had "... truste of any grounde ...".[23] Strong measures were called for: the English removed from their camp which was on the same side of the river Till as the Scots' camp, crossed the river, and encamped at Barmer Wood where they took counsel.

It was the eve of the great battle. The English were now only two miles distant from the Scots. At the council of war the English adopted a strategy that, combined with fortuitous circumstances, would win the day on the morrow. With the advice of his council, Surrey decided to execute a semi-circular flanking movement which would draw the Scots from their eminence on the Cheviot and precipitate a battle. The plan was to march toward the English citadel at Berwick, as if the English were giving up the fight, and then at a critical moment to take a left turn, cross the Till in two places — at Twizel Bridge and at a ford near Ford castle — and put themselves behind James and between him and Scotland. By electing to cross the Till in two different places, the Lord Admiral at Twizell Bridge and Surrey at a lower ford, Surrey

21 Hall, pp. 102-04; *L. P.*, I, 2246.
22 Hall, pp. 104-05.
23 *Ibid.*, p. 105.

was adopting the usually dangerous practice of dividing his army in the face of a superior enemy. His main objective was to outflank James and to persuade him that a serious attempt was being made to cut off both his supply lines and his line of retreat. The plan depended on deception and surprise. In order to deceive the Scots, it was necessary that James be thoroughly convinced that the English were retreating to Berwick. For this purpose the English were careful to make a great show and, except for the time of the actual crossing of the Till, they were viewed by the Scots.[24] The element of surprise consisted in James being suddenly confronted by the English now on the same side of the Till as he and in Surrey's departure from his son's route. If James could trust Surrey to be following in the Admiral's footsteps, he would have been drawing up the rear and James might have an immediate advantage in choosing to fight the son before the father arrived. But Surrey had a surprise for James, he did not elect to cross the Till by Twizell Bridge, but crossed it at a lower ford and, thus, was able to bring his forces almost up to a straight line with those of his son.

The Lord Admiral broke camp at five o'clock in the morning and crossed Twizell Bridge at eleven o'clock. His father did not leave until considerably later in the day. Since the Admiral had the artillery with him,[25] it may have taken him longer to make the march. When James learned of the English maneuvre, he took counsel and determined to leave his own position. He may have been making for the Scottish border when he was surprised by the appearance of the English, or he may merely have wished to get to Branxton moor before the English took it. At any rate, he ordered his forces to move some time after being informed that the English van had crossed the Till. Fire was set to the refuse, creating a smoke screen of sorts, and

---

[24] *Ibid.*, pp. 105-07; Charles Oman, *A History Of The Art Of War In The Sixteenth Century* (London, 1937), p. 307. Credit for this strategy of making a feigned retreat to Berwick and then a surprise attack by use of a flanking movement has been given by two authors to Surrey's son Thomas. Brenan, *House of Howard*, I, 98; Dallaway-Cartwright, II, pt. 2, 197. As far as it can be determined from contemporary evidence, the decision was, as in Hall, made in a council of war. As commander of the English forces, Surrey deserves credit for the victory. Recently an article largely based on Col. Leather's account of Flodden appeared in *History Today* in which the author, Sir John McEwen speculates that the decision to cross the Till at a different place than Twizell Bridge was made independently by Surrey who had not even informed his son of his intention. Sir John McEwen, "The Battle Of Flodden, September 9th, 1513", *History Today*, VIII (1958), 337-46.

[25] Hall, p. 107; *L. P.*, I, 2246.

the Scots broke camp.[26] The Scots were successful in reaching the top of the moor before the English. It was now almost four o'clock in the afternoon and both armies were tired after their forced marches. But once again, James had the high ground and if it were not for a lucky accident or two, he might not have fought.

While James was contemplating the English movements, Lord Edmund Howard was suddenly sighted by Lord Hume, the Scottish commander of James's left brigade. With scarcely any thought given to the consequences of his action, Hume attacked. He and his men bore down on Edmund Howard whose force of three thousand men was greatly outnumbered. Hume swept all before him; Howard was felled three times as he bravely tried to stem the impetus of Hume's charge. Howard's soldiers, predominantly Lancashire and Cheshire men, soon gave up the fight, turned their backs, and fled with Hume's borderers in close pursuit. The pursuit did not end until the Scots had captured and spoiled the English camp. Hume sat out the rest of the fight, thinking the Scots had won.[27] Timely assistance sent to Edmund by his father did not prevent the Scots from going through the English line as if it were paper, but aid given by Lord Dacre did save Edmund from capture and made it possible to reform the remnants of his force into some kind of order. For the English, the significance of the first engagement was found in Lord Hume's absenting himself from the remainder of the fight. Even if Hume had wished to regroup his forces, supposing that he knew the battle still continued, it would have been practically impossible, for his men were far more interested in booty than in fighting.

When Lord Thomas Howard had seen his brother's men being overwhelmed, and his own position threatened by the forces of the Earls of Crawford and Montrose, he had ripped off the Agnus Dei from his neck and sent it to his father with the message that his situation was desperate. Surrey had then despatched the commander of his right wing, Lord Dacre, to help Edmund. As quickly as he could, the old earl drew his forces into a line with those of Lord Thomas. Still the battle was fought in pieces, rather than in one big melee. There were four engagements with Edmund opposing Lord Hume; Lord Thomas, the Earls of Crawford and Montrose; Surrey,

[26] W. Mackay Mackenzie, *The Secret Of Flodden* (Edinburgh, 1931), p. 43. Leather, p. 11.
[27] Mackenzie, p. 45; Leather, pp. 48-51; *L. P.*, I, 2246; James Gairdner (ed.), *Three Fifteenth-Century Chronicles* (= Camden Society, N. S. No. 28) London, 1880), p. 88. Hereafter cited as *Fifteenth Century Chronicles*.

James; and Sir Edward Stanley, the Earls of Argyle and Lennox. As it turned out, this arrangement distinctly favored Surrey. He and the other English captains stayed in the rear[28] and let the soldiers do most of the fighting, and did not, unless forced by circumstances, personally lead their men in battle as did James. This meant that Surrey was able to use his military intelligence to reinforce weak spots in his line and to attempt, when the opportunity presented itself, to turn James's flanks. For example, when Lord Thomas successfully defeated the forces of Montrose and Crawford, he attacked James's force which was locked in a vicious struggle with his father. The same was true of Sir Edward Stanley who, though the last to begin fighting, finished in time to send his men to attack the enemy in the rear.[29]

Artillery played a key role in the battle. It was the accurate English bombardment of James and his men which forced the Scots to come down from the hill. They descended, strung out in four brigades, each within bow shot of one another. This accounted for fighting the battle as if it were four separate engagements. The king of the Scots saw what was happening to Edmund Howard and took heart from it. He thought that one good charge would turn the battle into a rout. As quickly as possible he threw himself from his horse, grabbed a weapon and strode into the thickest of the fighting. The flower of the Scottish nobility followed him and died at his side. James, himself, was killed fighting within a spear's length of Surrey.[30] James's proximity to Surrey shows how desperate the fighting really was and how close James came to victory. In fact, only a spear's thrust away — for if Surrey were in the rear directing his men, then James very nearly penetrated the entire depth of the English line. If James could

[28] Hall, pp. 107-10; L. P., I, 2246, 2578. Though Hall says that Dacre did not fight during the battle, the "Articles of Battle" (L. P., I, 2246), contradicts him at this point. See also Fifteenth Century Chronicles, p. 88, which tells of Dacre's timely rescue. Since Dacre's men were on horseback (R. L. Mackie, p. 252) and not on foot, as were the majority of English troops, his task was made much easier. Being on foot meant that the English march prior to the battle is more likely to have been a distance of eight miles as Mackie affirms and not the fifteen which Mackenzie states.

[29] L. P., I, 2246; Hall, p. 110; Polydore Vergil, p. 219.

[30] Ibid., 219-21; L. P., I, 2246; Hall, pp. 107-08. Hall states that the English gunners were far more effective than the Scots who did no harm with their guns. In fact, he relates that the English master gunner slew the master gunner of Scotland. Hall, p. 108. R. L. Mackie follows Hall's account and adds the information that James's foreign gunners were not at the battlefield but aboard ship. R. L. Mackie, pp. 263-75.

have pushed the English back a little further, he would have pushed them into the bog which was at their back.[31]

Instead of victory, the Scots found defeat and, in many cases, death. The fifteen foot spears with which they fought were no match for the eight foot English bills which cleaved off the dangerous spear heads, leaving the Scots dependent on their short swords for defense. And, of course, the short swords, though good for close fighting, did not have the range of the bill. In addition, the hilly terrain was not suitable to fighting in the Swiss type of phalanx where the long spear is most effective.[32] Fighting, as they did on an incline, did not give them the opportunity to get their spears set. Though they fought bravely, the English had superior weapons and the Scots succumbed one by one. When Lord Thomas, Dacre, and Stanley closed in on James's force, an English victory was virtually assured.

With the death of the Scottish king and his chief nobles, the battle became one great scene of carnage. The English slew as they pleased and pursued those who thought to save life rather than sell honor dear. They chased the fleeing Scots for three miles and would have slain even more had they been on horseback. Ten thousand Scots were killed while the English lost but four hundred men. It is said that there was not a noble family in Scotland that did not sustain some loss at Flodden. With the battle over, the English began to task of consolidating their victory by collecting the enemy's ordinance. While engaged in this operation, Lord Thomas Howard and his men were set upon by eight hundred Scots and a furious skirmish ensued in which Howard won the day, killing two hundred Scots. As usual, Howard's father, the circumspect earl, awaited further instructions before making final disposition of the large number of prisoners taken at Flodden, decreeing that no gentleman prisoner should leave until Henry's pleasure was known. He also awaited Henry's pleasure as to what to do with James's body. The bruised and pierced body of the Scottish king had been found after the bloody battle and brought to Surrey who treated it with all the respect due to a king. The body was taken to the nearest church, then to Berwick, and finally to Richmond.[33]

---

[31] Leather, p. 61.
[32] *L. P.*, I, 2283; Mackenzie, pp. 76-91.
[33] *Fifteen Century Chronicles*, pp. 88-89; *L. P.*, I, 2246, 2268, 2270, 2286. For a list of the Scottish nobles who were killed see G. E. C., V, Appendix D. Mackie says the English losses were 1500. R. L. Mackie, p. 268. Since James died excom-

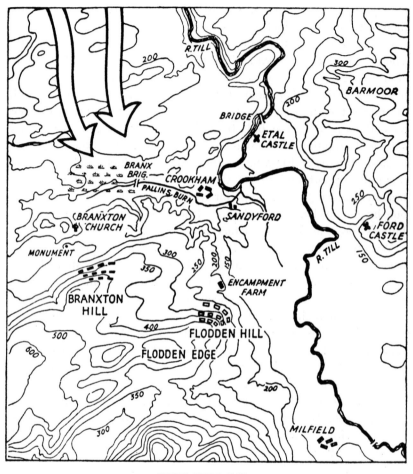

VERTICAL INTERVAL 50 FT.

THE BATTLE OF FLODDEN

 English approach march

 Approximate locations of first

 and second Scottish positions

With the general demoralization fostered by their defeat, the Scots were not prepared to meet any concerted offensive made by the English. Obviously, the time was propitious for a large scale English offensive. It was Henry's wish that the English advantage should be followed up. He instructed Lord Dacre, warden of the marches, to make two raids on Scotland through the West and Middle Marches and likewise ordered Lord Darcy, the steward of the lordships of Pontefract and Knaresburgh, to attack through the East March. But Dacre foresaw difficulties and problems similar to those encountered by Surrey when the earl had attempted a raid on Tevydale in the war of 1497. Furthermore, the warden saw a possible weakening of his forces in the Middle Marches if he were forced to contribute to a raid on the East.[34] And in passing, he mentioned the quality of his fighting men who "... fled at the first shot of the Scottish guns...".[35] The mopping-up operations and prosecution of the border war were left not to Surrey but to Dacre. Apparently Surrey's special commission as Lieutenant-General of the North permitted him only to repel the Scots. Once he had defeated them, his job was done.

Any mention of Flodden inevitably leads to questions about the secret of Surrey's success. Was he indeed, as one author suggests, another Hannibal, who won because he was a superior general?[36] Certainly it does seem strange that James could not have beaten an inferior force which he at one time, at any rate, had tactically out-maneuvered. To Polydore Vergil, Henry's historian, there was no secret in James's defeat. James's rashness and excess courage brought about his own downfall. When he elected to fight in the front of his men rather than to direct military operations from the rear as did Surrey,[37] he had, in effect, lost the battle. The Scots themselves held James responsible for their disastrous defeat[38] and indicated that his leadership left much to be desired. Edward Hall attributes Surrey's success to both strategy and superiority of the English artillery which precipitated the contest by forcing the Scots to fight or be cannonaded

---

municate for having broken his treaty with the English, it was necessary to get special permission to bury him. Ellis, *Letters*, I, 92. The Scottish ordinance collected after the battle amounted to five curtalls, two culvereins, four sacres, and six serpentines. Hall, p. 112.

[34] *L. P.*, I, 2382, 2386, 2505.
[35] *Ibid.*, 2386.
[36] Leather, p. 24.
[37] Polydore Vergil, pp. 219-21.
[38] *L. P.*, I, 2578.

in their tracks.[39] Bishop Ruthal, in reporting the conflict, noted that the English bills beat the long spears of the Scots.[40] To a great extent modern historians reconstructing the battle have followed one or more of the contemporary accounts with a bit of imaginative embellishment here and there. Colonel Leather has given most of the credit for the victory to Surrey's strategy and to the part played by Sir Edward Stanley's brigade which acted as a decoy while the Howards, with the major part of the English forces, made the circling and flanking movement. Leather's reconstruction, though interesting, seems to emphasize too much the element of surprise and secrecy in Surrey's strategy.[41] When the English broke camp, they wished to make the Scots think that they really were taking the road to Berwick. They had to be seen by the Scots for this purpose, and Hall says that for most of the period prior to the battle, the Scots were watching the English. And when Twizell Bridge was crossed, the Scots learned of this almost immediately. This was surprise enough for James, and he was forced by this new development to take counsel with his captains. His delay in doing anything about the English advance contributed to his unorganized state of affairs and later he was rudely shocked by the sight of all the English forces before him.

On the other hand, Mr. W. M. MacKenzie chooses to emphasize the critical role of weapons in the story of Flodden. He embroiders Ruthal's modest statement about the superiority of the eight foot English bill over the fifteen foot Scottish spear into a clever tale of the carnage wrought by the vastly superior bill.[42] However, the most recent historian of Flodden, Mr. R. L. Mackie, after carefully assessing the evidence, determines that the secret of Flodden is not lodged in one weapon or in the strategy, but in a combination of many things. He cites the English as having superior leadership, soldiers, artillery, weapons, and skill. He rather ruefully comments that Surrey was accompanied by five hundred armed men who were no strangers to war and notes the one thousand trained men brought by the Lord

---

[39]   Hall, pp. 106-08.
[40]   L. P., I, 2283. According to Ruthal, archery did not play a decisive role in the battle, since the Scots wore such heavy armor. Leather's account, however, states that a barrage of English arrows was responsible for cutting down the force of the Earls of Argylle and Lennox and also for initiating the final engagement between James and Surrey. The French ambassador, De la Motte, died while fighting for Lennox and Argylle. Leather, pp. 55-61.
[41]   Ibid., pp. 9, 24, 55.
[42]   Mackenzie, pp. 89-91.

Admiral. Actually, Surrey's men were his gentlemen and tenants and in no case should be considered to have had much more training than James's shire levies.[43] It was customary for each nobleman to call his retainers to the king's standard, as in the case of the Earl of Oxford prior to the Battle of Stoke or the Duke of Norfolk before Bosworth. Normally these men were not soldiers. Of course, in the case of the Lord Admiral's men many of them would probably have preferred to face the Scots than their commander who relentlessly goaded them on from the rear. Thomas Howard, junior, was a ferociously efficient fighting man. Earlier in the summer he instructed the king's council to hang several of the men who had run away from his service and to keep the remainder in Hereford jail until he could personally see to their execution.[44]

None of the accounts, either contemporary or modern, emphasizes sufficiently the role of chance in the battle. The thanks offered to God and to the English saints may in some way be construed as a realization that the English had, indeed, been very fortunate. Fighting the battle piecemeal, as it were, gave the English a distinct advantage, and the removal of Hume's borderers from the contest at an early hour also favored them. Nor must the crucial work of Dacre, Lord Thomas Howard, and Stanley be forgotten, for their attack on James's rear and flank assured an English victory. Surrey was fortunate in the way things turned out — it could have gone badly for him. He was a desperate man with troops who needed food and drink, and he took desperate measures. No adversary is more dangerous than one who is almost beaten, for he will try anything to win. Though much of the credit for the victory belongs to the skill of the English gunners and the efficient way in which the English used their bills, Surrey deserves to be remembered as the commander responsible for a winning strategy.

[43] R. L. Mackie, pp. 274-76; Hall, p. 96. R. L. Mackie also thinks that Surrey broke his word by not fighting James at the time appointed by the heralds and thus, gained an advantage through deceit. R. L. Mackie, p. 273.

[44] L. P., I, 1978.

VI

DUKE AND DIPLOMAT

Accidents in history are indeed strange. Surrey the seventy year old military expert, who was denied the opportunity to share in Henry VIII's French triumphs, won acclaim at Flodden that overshadowed that of his royal master. Even the king's wife twitted her husband about the disparity between what was done to the Scots and what Henry was doing in France. She sent Henry "... the piece of the King of Scots coat which John Glyn now bringeth. In this your Grace shall see how I can keep my promys, sending you for your banners a King's coat".[1] The primary fact about the battle, which eluded no one, was James's death which, if nothing else could, convinced all of the smashing victory won by Surrey. The death of a king in battle, though an occasional occurrence in the days of the later middle ages, was still enough of a rarity to cause comment and excite wonder. Almost immediately, Surrey's performance became the subject of a poem inappropriately titled "Skelton Laureate Against The Scottes". In it the vainglorious John Skelton, the most famous of Tudor poets, described how Surrey, identified as the White Lion because of his use of the white lion badge of his ancestors, the Mowbray dukes of Norfolk, killed James, the Red Lion.

> At Branxston more and Flodden hylles,
> Our Englysh bowes, our Englysh bylles,
> Agaynt you gaue so sharpe a shower,
> That of Scotland ye lost the flower.
> The Whyte Lyon, there rampaunte of moode,
> He ragyd and rent out your hart bloode;
> He the Whyte, and ye the Red,
> The Whyte there slew the Red starke ded.[2]

[1] *L. P.*, I, 2268.
[2] Alexander Dyce (ed.), *The Poetical Works Of John Skelton*, 2 vols. (London, 1843), I, 186.

Inaccurate as to the relative importance of English archery at the engagement, Skelton's lines express little more than a crude metaphor of the killing of the king. But in its own way the Skeltonic picture is effective, for it seemed to identify the durable earl with an unrestrained ferocity that some call bravery. To Surrey's contemporaries, his badge, that of the lion, indicated the earl's superb qualities as a warrior, for the strength, courage, and noble bearing of the lion are proverbial. Surrey's grandson, the famous poet Henry Howard, earl of Surrey, also chose to remember his grandfather in the attitude of a savage beast literally tearing his enemy to pieces. Upon being refused a dance by a lady at court, he wrote a poem in which he exclaimed:

> How can ye thus intreat a Lion of the race,
> That with his paws a crowned king devoured in the place.
> Whose nature is to prey upon no simple food,
> As long as he may suck the flesh, and drink of noble blood.[3]

No one underestimated the magnitude of Surrey's feat. In one magnificent engagement he had established the superiority of English arms, beaten the Scots decisively and left them leaderless, and secured his own fame as a brilliant general. Though he had participated in many battles: Barnet, Bosworth, Ackworth, and even fought for the illustrious Charles the Bold of Burgundy, his military reputation was forged at Flodden. Hitherto recognized primarily for his steady, competent if unimaginative service to the crown, he made the most of his one big opportunity as a commanding general. He moved his forces with the sure touch of an old campaigner and added to this wisdom in battle a dash of the audacity and recklessness of a far younger man. Though he was seventy, he had a vigorous mind and willing agents to do what he could not do himself. His desperate attempt to force James into battle proved successful as he thought it would, and counting on his knowledge of James's character, he was able to take advantage of his opponent's excess of courage. His victory was a personal victory as well as an English triumph over a foreign enemy. He had matched wits with James, and James had lost both the battle and his life.

Soon after the encounter at Flodden, Surrey took James's body with him to York where he was met by his wife who had stayed at the Archdeacon of York's residence during the campaign. Surrey, his wife,

---

[3] *The Poems Of Henry Howard Earl Of Surrey* (London, n. d.), p. 49.

and his retinue were treated to a royal feast by the mayor of the city before leaving for London. Whereas he had set out for the North grimly determined to make James pay a heavy price for his missing the French adventure, Surrey now returned as a celebrated general. Perhaps, as the recorder of the York House Book wrote "GODE WAS HIS GUYDE",[4] but even if this were so, then the old earl should be treated to respect and honor as His earthly representative. Both countryside and court buzzed with the news of his achievement, talked incessantly of his valor, and wondered what his reward would be. Of course, Catherine took great delight in Surrey's prowess, for the defeat of the Scots cast lustre upon the way in which she maintained the realm in her husband's absence. Though she might tease Henry about her accomplishments, she knew that it would not do to outdo her spouse, and she wisely joined in the current refrain that Surrey's victory was made possible by God. She wrote to Wolsey that: "This matier is soo marvelous that it semeth to bee of Godds doing aloone. I trust the King shal remember to thanke hym for it. . . ."[5] Whether or not the victory came from God alone, the people and courtiers were talking about Surrey's part in it. The importance of his act was such that many thought him worthy of a dukedom. Thomas Ruthal, the bishop of Durham, wrote to Wolsey expressing his sincere belief that Surrey did indeed deserve a dukedom and that the other English nobles present at Flodden should receive special letters of thanks from the king.[6] Popular imagination demanded that the faithful old earl, the white lion of the North, be rewarded for his deed. In a council meeting at Westminster it was decided to make Surrey duke of Norfolk for his service against the Scots and his son, Thomas, earl of Surrey. At the same time that the Howards were to receive their reward, it was thought fitting to create Charles Brandon, duke of Suffolk, and Charles Somerset, earl of Worcester, for the military service which they had rendered in the French campaign.

In a magnificent ceremony at Lambeth on Candlemas Day, the Garter King of Arms gave the four men the patents of their new office. Of course, Henry, the most important nobles, assorted gentlemen, and a multitude of people were there — so many, in fact, that one could scarcely draw breath. Dressed in a resplendent gown of crimson velvet, Surrey became the new Duke of Norfolk, while his

---

[4] Raine, CVI, 42.
[5] Ellis, *Letters*, I, 90.
[6] *L. P.*, I, 2284.

son received his former dignity.[7] The new duke also obtained a special addition to his coat of arms, ". . . on a bend on the shield of Howard a demilion gules, pierced in the mouth with an arrow, and colored according to the arms of Scotland, as borne by the said King of the Scots".[8] In the realm of more tangible receipts he received besides the forty pound ducal annuity, thirty manors located in Salop, Warwick, Wiltshire, Berkshire, Hertsford, Oxford, Kent, Derby, and Nottingham. His son, the new Earl of Surrey, received a twenty pound annuity plus lands which amounted to sixteen manors, two castles, and a rent.[9]

Two questions arise in connection with Surrey's elevation to the dukedom of Norfolk: first, was his creation a restoration to the grant which his father held in 1483? Second, did his new rank in any way increase his power at court? According to J. H. Round, the present Dukes of Norfolk inherit the dukedom under the creation of 1514 and not that of 1483.[10] Technically, this is correct, since the grant of 1514 did not include all the powers granted to John Howard and included the new addition. Thus, the new creation was not a restoration to his father's title. However, since Thomas Howard is the second Howard to bear the title of Duke of Norfolk, it has been customary to designate him as the second Duke of Norfolk rather than the first Duke of Norfolk of the second Howard creation. This designation, though not palatable to the genealogist or the peerage historian, is valuable since it makes Thomas Howard readily identifiable as the Howard who next became Duke of Norfolk after John Howard, the first duke.

As a duke, Thomas Howard joined a very select group. There were only three in the kingdom: Charles Brandon, the new duke of Suffolk, Edward Stafford, duke of Buckingham, and himself. Buckingham represented the old nobility, having an ancestry which went back to Edward III, while Brandon was the son of a mere knight. Buckingham was born to the purple — both his father and great-grandfather had preceded him in his dignity as duke — while Charles Brandon by dint of his military skill and popularity with his sovereign won royal advancement: first, as a Spear in Henry VIII's newly formed corps of gentlemen guards, then as a viscount, and finally as a duke. Bucking-

---

[7] Polydore Vergil, p. 223; Mackie, pp. 277-79; Charles W. Ferguson, *Naked To Mine Enemies: The Life of Cardinal Wolsey* (Boston, 1958), p. 106; B. M. Egerton, 985, fols. 60 (v), 61 (r).

[8] *L. P.*, I, 2684 (1).

[9] *Ibid.*, 2684 (2).

[10] J. H. Round, *Studies in the Peerage*, p. 109.

ham was much nearer to the throne than either the new Dukes of Norfolk and Suffolk. His descent from the fifth son of Edward III gave him a claim in some sense superior to that of Henry VII who was descended from the bastard son of John of Gaunt, Edward III's fourth son.[11] In the event of Henry VIII's decease without heirs, Buckingham was one of the logical claimants for the throne. Neither Norfolk nor Suffolk were that close to the succession. Norfolk's own position was midway between that of Buckingham and Suffolk. His family was ennobled a generation sooner than Brandon's and had achieved great place at Richard III's court when the Brandons were still gentry. Just as Norfolk, though, could look at Brandon as an upstart, a parvenu, and as one having come only lately to the royal banquet table, Buckingham could recall that his family were nobles many generations sooner than the Howards.

Some of Norfolk's joy in his new creation may have been dulled by Henry's decision to advance Brandon and Somerset, the Lord Chamberlain, to the new dignities of Duke of Suffolk and Earl of Worcester. While he was rewarding the Howards for their success at Flodden, Henry probably felt it agreeable, nay almost mandatory, to promote the military commanders of his van and rear, Brandon and Somerset, respectively. After all, even if not all were aware of it, he had had a fairly successful campaign in France, and these new creations would serve to jog men's memories. What may have seemed most bitter to the Howard faction in Brandon's creation was that there but for the grace of God might have gone the late Edward Howard. Small solace to the new Duke of Norfolk were his protégé Alexander Barclay's lines:

> Tell me frayle fortune, why did thous breuiate
> The liuing season of suche a captayne, [Edward Howard]
> That when his actes ought to be laureate
> Thy fauor turned him suffring to be slayne?
> I blame thee fortune and thee excuse agayne,
> For though thy fauour to him was rigorous,
> Suche is thy custome for to be vncertayne,
> And namely when man is hye and glorious.
> But moste worthy duke [Norfolk] hye and victorious,
> Respire to comfort, see the vncertentie
> Of other princes, whose fortune properous
> Oftetime haue ended in hard aduersite. . . .[12]

[11] G. E. C., XII, pt. 1, 454-51; D. N. B., XVIII, 854; James Gairdner, Henry The Seventh (London, 1892), pp. 2-3.
[12] Eclogues of Barclay, pp. 177-78.

At least the duke, who appears to Barclay as the very flower of chivalry and is honored by being selected as the governor of Barclay's imaginary Tower of Virtue which all knights strive to enter by worthy deeds, could comfort himself that his son died nobly in a just cause. In fact, the manner of Edward's death was to be an example to the entire nation.[13] And so the poet concludes:

> So duke most doughty ioy may that noble tree,
> Whose braunches honour shall neuer fade ne [nor] fall,
> While beast is on earth or fishes in the sea.[14]

Although Barclay's verses must have been very flattering to Norfolk, they could not take the place of his son. His loss and that of Sir Thomas Knyvett amounted to a disastrous blow to the Howard hopes for controlling king and council. Though his new dignity as a duke enhanced his social prestige and the Flodden land grant increased his revenues, power as always revolved around the person of the king and those who held his confidence. Charles Brandon took the place of Edward Howard as the convivial comrade-in-arms to the king, and the Howard direct contact with Henry was severely limited. Whether Brandon could be gained for the Howard faction was a moot point in 1514, but it seemed, even then, more likely that he would cast his lot with Wolsey.

As yet the extent of Wolsey's power was not evident. The ultimate question of who would influence the king was still in doubt. The triumvirate of Chancellor, Treasurer, and Privy Seal, as usual, controlled most of the crown's administrative detail and directed much of English foreign policy. But as early as March of 1514 it seemed that some changes were going to be made in the composition of this committee with Warham and Fox losing their places to Wolsey, the new bishop of Lincoln, and Ruthal, for a letter from Lord Dacre to council was addressed: "To my Lord of Norfolk's grace, my Lord Winchester, Lord Duresme [Ruthal], my Lord elect to Lincoln and other my Lords of the King's most honorable council."[15] While Henry's military commanders were sporting the ensigns of their new creations, Wolsey shed his office of almoner on his appointment to the bishopric of Lincoln. In addition, he received the bishopric of Tournai *in commendam* and on the death of Christopher Bainbridge, the archbishop of York, in the summer of 1514, he was advanced to that

[13] *Ibid.*, pp. 170-79.
[14] *Ibid.*, p. 179.
[15] *L. P.*, I, 2718.

prelate's office.[16] Clearly, he too was rewarded for the efficient manner in which he managed Henry's French expedition. Though the French in 1514 underestimated Wolsey's power by giving Norfolk a pension of one thousand thirty crowns which was thirty crowns more than Wolsey's, they would not make that mistake again. After Wolsey became chancellor in 1515, they increased his pension and during the later years spiced his take annually with an extra 6,000 livres.[17]

Great things were in store for Wolsey: the office of chancellor, a cardinal's hat, and a legateship *a latere*. By dint of hard work and almost superhuman energy, he rose to a position where he was indispensable to his king. During his illness of 1518 the government of England was immobilized.[18] His capacity for paper work was almost unbelievable, certainly to be compared favorably with that of Queen Elizabeth I's great minister, Lord Burghley. Cavendish tells the story of Wolsey getting up at four o'clock in the morning on one occasion to do a little paper work and not leaving his desk until his work was through at four o'clock in the afternoon.[19] Wolsey's former superior, Bishop Fox, was gravely concerned about the effect of overwork on Wolsey and admonished him to lay aside all work by six in the evening.[20] His strength, energy, dedication, and ability to master thousands of details made Wolsey a formidable adversary, indeed, for Norfolk. As a result of the French success, Wolsey was in a commanding position. The contest, if it can be called that, between the two men would be determined in the handling of England's diplomacy. Already it might seem though, that attempts of the Howards to frustrate Wolsey's designs were futile, and that though Norfolk had won his battle with the Scots, he had lost his war with Wolsey.

The diplomatic situation in 1514 was clear: England and Spain were allies in a war against France. Further, the allies were united by a marriage treaty which promised to join the English king's sister Mary to Charles, the heir to the Spanish throne. The two nations were participants in the Holy League, an alliance composed of Spain, England, the Holy Roman Empire, and the papacy which was directed against French aims in the Italian peninsula. For England's contribution to this alliance, the pope conferred his cap and sword of main-

---

[16]   Pollard, *Wolsey*, pp. 20-21.
[17]   *L. P.*, I, 3502; *C. S. P. Span.*, II, 273, 277, 305, 331; Pollard, *Wolsey*, p. 102.
[18]   *L. P.*, II, 3372.
[19]   Cited by Ferguson, pp. 122-23.
[20]   *L. P.*, II, 1814.

tenance on Henry VIII.[21] Although no rupture between the two major powers in the alliance was apparent, there were murmurings that all was not well within the alliance — even the English councillors were talking. As early as April 17 Fox had noted to Wolsey that he did not think Charles would go through with the planned marriage.[22] With the following month came the astounding news that the wily Ferdinand had made a separate truce with France in direct contravention of his pact with England. Henry VIII's councillors were mortified, nettled, and enraged; Ferdinand's perfidy touched them deeply. It was not merely that the solid alliance constructed by Norfolk and the other councillors should be shattered, but that their king had been insulted. Ferdinand had treated Henry like a boy,[23] like a callow youth unschooled in the ways of the world and the mysteries of international diplomacy.

Ferdinand's betrayal of his son-in-law made a lasting impression. Never again would the English king find himself in quite so embarrasing a situation. The public reaction was instantaneous, a disavowal of the Anglo-Spanish alliance was called for, and with amazing rapidity a diplomatic *volte-face* was achieved. On July 30 Norfolk was one of the witnesses to Princess Mary's renunciation of her marriage compact; on August 2 Norfolk, Fox, and Wolsey were commissioned to seek a marriage alliance with France and to renew the treaties of Etaples and London; and on August 13 Norfolk had the pleasure of being one of the witnesses to the notorial instrument proclaiming Mary's espousal to the French king, Louis XII. The treaty of Paris was confirmed in September and plans were made for conducting Mary to France under the care of Norfolk.[24] Specific instructions were given to the duke as to procedure, to the dowry, and to the delivery of the princess's person. The initial payment of the dowry amounting to 200,000 crowns was not to be delivered until the marriage ceremony was celebrated. Even the size of each noble's retinue was strictly prescribed for attendance at the wedding: the duke was to be allowed to have as much livery as two earls and earls as much as two barons and barons as much as four knights. Once the wedding had been performed, Norfolk was to take care of the new Queen's servant situation, that is, to see that she had a suitable staff and then depart.[25]

[21] *L. P.*, I, 2929.
[22] *Ibid.*, 2811.
[23] *Ibid.*, 3018.
[24] *Ibid.*, 3101, 3111, 3146, 3269, 3324 (33).
[25] *Ibid.*, 3294, 3324 (33), 3354.

Inevitably Norfolk's commission to conduct Mary to France brings to mind a similar duty he executed for her sister Margaret. In both cases Norfolk managed to arouse each sister's wrath. Margaret had disliked Norfolk intensely because he had isolated her and her councillors from her husband and had used the occasion to worm himself into the Scottish king's good graces. Margaret's reaction had been a combination of bewilderment and hurt pride. She threw herself on the mercies of her father, apparently without avail. Mary's reaction to Norfolk's dismissal of her English servants was more explosive and characteristically more worthy of the famous Tudor temperament. Writing to Henry on October 12, she described how: "On the morn next after my marriage my chamberlain, with all other men servants, were discharged, [an]d likewise my mother Guldeford, with other my women and maidens, except such as never had experience nor knowledge how to advertise or give me counsel in any time of need, which is to be feared more shortly than your grace thought at the time of my departing, as my mother Guldeford can more plainly show your grace than I can write. . . . I marvel much that my Lord of Norfolk wold at all times so lightly grant everything at their requests here . . . would God my Lord of Zorke [York] had come with me in the room of my Lord of Norfolk, for (the)n am I sure I should have been left much more at my heart's (ease) than I am now."[26] And she also took the liberty of writing about her plight "To my loving friend the Abp of Zorke".[27] Charles Brandon, duke of Suffolk, also wrote to Wolsey, the new archbishop of York, spelling out for him the political implications of Norfolk's action — that the Queen's servants had been released because they were of Wolsey's appointment and not of the choosing of Norfolk and his son Surrey.[28]

Actually, Norfolk was in difficult position. Mary kept herself continually surrounded by her English retainers and the omnipresent Lady Guldeford never left her side. It was plain that Louis, the doddering old king of France, could not be alone with his young bride. He complained about the situation to Norfolk and insisted that the ubiquitous Lady Guldeford and other servants be removed.[29] Norfolk complied with the king's request as would any intelligent courtier. He really did not have much choice and if the removal of

---

[26] L. P., I, 3355.

[27] Ibid., 3356.

[28] Ibid., 3376.

[29] Green, Lives of the Princesses, V, 45-47.

these attendants satisfied his resentment of Wolsey's management of the French marriage, so much the better. Perhaps the duke was too much in the habit of acquiescing to royal demands to assert his lady's rights, and maybe he thought that the young queen was protesting too much about her new responsibilities to an old man. Mary need not have been too concerned about her May-December marriage, for Louis died on January 1, 1515 after a scant eighty day marriage.[30] The romantic story of Mary's flight from France and her marriage to Suffolk is too well-known to need retelling. Contrary to Polydore Vergil's supposition that Henry VIII had contemplated making Brandon a member of his family, and with this in mind, had elevated him to a dukedom[31] and later ordered him to marry Mary, it seems that Henry was genuinely displeased and even angered by the marriage. He made Mary and Suffolk pay heavily for the privilege of their marriage: £24,000 was to be given to the king in yearly installments of £1,000; Mary's dowry was also forfeit to the king; her plate, her jewels, and the wardship of the Lady Lisle were similarly surrendered.[32] While the king only insisted on pecuniary penalties, the king's council and the English people cried for more drastic measures. Some councillors thought Suffolk deserved death for his action, others merely suggested an indefinite imprisonment, and the English people called for his blood. Suffolk dared not leave the king's house for fear that the English tradesmen aroused by his presumptuous act would tear him to pieces.[33] The storm over Henry's favorite sister's love marriage, however, soon subsided, and the Venetian ambassador could write as early as August 5, 1515 that Suffolk was in favor and held power only a little less than that wielded by the king himself.[34]

The whole affair did not weaken Norfolk's position at court and during the year 1515 he played an active part in the formulation of his country's diplomacy. The international situation was tense: all powers waited to see what the new king of France, Francis I, would do. Both Maximilian, the Holy Roman Emperor, and Ferdinand, that most Catholic king, lingered on the scene while Charles, the grandson of each, awaited his opportunity to rule in their places. Ferdinand disliked his grandson intensely because Charles's coming of age meant

---

[30]   Polydore Vergil, p. 225.
[31]   *Ibid.*, 223, 229.
[32]   *L. P.*, II, 436.
[33]   *Ibid.*, 367, 399.
[34]   *Ibid.*, 784.

that the youth would lay claim to the government of the richest of all Spanish provinces, Castile, and Charles was in Maximilian's pocket.

There was still peace. A new peace with France had been engineered by Norfolk, Wolsey, and Fox, and confirmed by Francis I on May 8, 1515.[35] The traditional English alliance with Spain was in abeyance until such time as the warlike, energetic Francis broke his treaty with the English or threatened the European balance of power by trying to win the hegemony of the Italian peninsula. One question more than all others tormented the Venetian ambassador as he made his rounds to the residences of the important English councillors, Norfolk, Wolsey, and Thomas Ruthal, Bishop of Durham, soon to become Lord Privy Seal: would the French cross the Alps and launch a new Italian campaign? Each of the councillors told the Ambassador that he did not think Francis would cross the Alps and even Henry VIII when asked for his opinion, gave out the same answer despite intelligence sent him in April that Francis was definitely going into Italy. In fact, Norfolk and Wolsey intimated to the Venetian in July that England could prevent Francis from taking a military force into Italy.[36] Francis's subsequent Italian campaign and his resounding victory at Marignano on September 13 gave Wolsey, a newly created Cardinal, some second thoughts as to what England could and could not do. His mortification at Francis's action may account for the vindictiveness with which he advanced in council his schemes for war against France by paying Maximilian and his troops to do the job. Although some of the wiser councillors, including Norfolk, were against Wolsey's personal vendetta, the cardinal carried out his project and Richard Pace was dispatched with sufficient money to the Emperor. But Wolsey's plan was frustrated in January 1517 when the impecunious Emperor, for a further financial consideration, withdrew his army and joined the alliance of Noyon which had originally been signed between Charles, now king of Spain, and Francis in July 1516.[37] This meant that the Emperor had changed sides — he was now the ally of Francis, the king of France.[38]

Though Wolsey did not carry all before him on the international scene, he did at home. While the extent of his power had not been evident to all in 1513 or 1514, it was blatantly so in 1515, and his

[35] *Ibid.*, 300, 301, 428.
[36] *Ibid.*, 343, 652, 666, 673; *C. S. P. Ven.*, II, 635.
[37] *Wolsey*, p. 55, 114; Polydore Vergil, 235.
[38] *L. P.*, II, 975, 1087.

creation as Lord Chancellor in Warham's place[39] confirmed the fact that he held first position amongst the king's councillors. During Brandon's personal crisis over his marriage, Wolsey extended his friendship to him and sheltered him from the worst of Henry's wrath.[40] Thus, Brandon became a fast friend and an active, enthusiastic supporter of the cardinal. Wolsey's supremacy in the council made opposition to him less likely than before for he now held a commanding post, not only as the unofficial chief advisor to the king, but as the first officer of state. By the end of October 1515, two months before his appointment as chancellor, Giustinian, the Venetian Ambassador, discerned that the whole power of the state rested with Wolsey, and he referred to him a short time later as *ipse rex*.[41]

The new cardinal and chancellor was not content to exercise his power discreetly. He insisted on all the prerogatives of his office and concentrated on impressing all with the extent of his magnificence and power. When he received his cardinal's hat, he capped its reception by a public ceremony at Westminster Abbey with all the highest officers of state, chief ecclesiastics, and nobles in attendance. At the end of the ceremony the cardinal was conducted by the Dukes of Norfolk and Suffolk to his palace at York Place. Moreover, the Cardinal affected golden cloth for his table, a golden chair, and a golden cushion for his chair. Wherever he went he was preceded by a servant bearing a symbol of his new authority and shouting: "Make way for the cardinal." By reason of this new honor he was entitled to have two crosses borne before him, since he was already entitled to one as the Archbishop of York. His new magnificence, if we are to believe Polydore Vergil, did not impress the other councillors or the English populace. The multitudes began to despise and fear him, whereas before they had loved and trusted him. After Wolsey's appointment as cardinal, Warham, the archbishop of Canterbury, never again had the cross of his office borne before him in Wolsey's presence.[42]

Already some of the older councillors had become disaffected and displeased with Wolsey's conduct of affairs. Polydore Vergil relates that Warham and Fox were among the first to leave the council,

---

[39] Warham surrendered the great seal on December 22 and Wolsey took the oath of office on December 24. *Ibid.*, 1335.
[40] Mandell Creighton, *Cardinal Wolsey* (London, 1888), p. 37.
[41] *L. P.*, II, 1086; Pollard, *Wolsey*, p. 102.
[42] Polydore Vergil, p. 231; *Wolsey*, pp. 56-57.

followed by Suffolk and later by Norfolk who retired to his country estate.[43] The Venetian ambassador ascribes the specific reason for Fox and Warham's departure to their dislike of Wolsey's policy of giving aid to Maximillian against Venice and France. Even the faithful Sir Thomas Lovell seemed to have withdrawn permanently from court.[44] Fox certainly had left court by April 1516, for Wolsey wrote to him in this month asking when he would be back. Fox's reply indicated that Wolsey could not count on him for duty at court since his spiritual responsibilities took all of his time. Fox had decided to have done with the affairs of kings and queens and devote himself to his neglected diocese and the salvation of his soul.[45] In view of the situation at court it was probably a very satisfying decision.

Lord Herbert of Cherbury has suggested that Norfolk left court because he was tired of trying to raise money for Henry's wars.[46] Actually, neither Lord Herbert nor Polydore Vergil are correct as to the reason why Norfolk left court. Between May and October of 1516 the duke was gravely ill, for at the end of May one of the Earl of Shrewsbury's correspondents remarked that Norfolk was sick and not expected to live.[47] That Norfolk was indeed ill seems to be borne out by an indenture made by his executors in August to raise a certain sum from his manors and lands for the making of his tomb.[48] The approach of death is often a strong impetus for setting one's affairs in order. Norfolk's absence from court was duly noted by the Venetian ambassador in October. The ambassanor observed that the duke, one of the managers of English diplomacy, had been absent for several months. Although ill and away from court, this does not mean that Norfolk opposed Wolsey and his control of the council, for in July, the same Venetian ambassador observed that: "To the dissatisfaction of everybody, the whole direction of affairs rests with the Cardinal, the Bishop of Durham [Thomas Ruthal], and the Lord Treasurer...."[49]

Obviously, Norfolk had made his peace with Wolsey, as other councillors had not. If he could not be chief minister, the duke was

[43] Polydore Vergil, pp. 231-32.
[44] C. S. P. Ven., II, 750.
[45] L. P., II, 1814.
[46] Edward, Lord Herbert of Cherbury, The History Of England Under Henry VIII (London, 1870), p. 164.
[47] L. P., II, 1959.
[48] John Harvey, English Medieval Architects: A Biographical Dictionary Down To 1550 Including Master Masons, Carpenters, Building Contractors and others responsible for Design (London, 1954), p. 286.
[49] C. S. P. Ven., 750.

still willing to exercise as much power as he was able. He had his own area of power in the moribund exchequer and in the control of customs appointments. He shared with Wolsey and Ruthal in the responsibility for the making of English policy. Though more often than not he deferred to the cardinal's will, the duke helped conduct his country's diplomacy. Far better to be active in the council than to be cast into the outer darkness of retirement to one's country estates. The duke, though a proud man, was never stimulated to the excesses of his son, Thomas, the earl of Surrey, who with the Marquis of Dorset was put out of the council chamber in 1516, for some unknown reason. And Surrey was a violent man who had once tried to stab Wolsey.[50] If nothing else, Norfolk had learned in his long life to make the most of his opportunities. When he saw that he could not control the situation, he accommodated himself to suit the man in control — Wolsey.

Despite his advancing age, the duke was more than a passive observer in the key events of his declining years. He especially relished being a diplomat. He was present with Wolsey, Ruthal, Richard Nix, the bishop of Norwich, Sir Thomas Lovell, and Sir Henry Marny when the Emperor Maximilian's representative, the Cardinal of Sion, came to the English court seeking aid against Venice and France.[51] Several days later, Giustinian, the Venetian ambassador, had an interview with Norfolk in which Norfolk showed himself in fine form. Quite naturally, Giustinian was worried about Cardinal Sion and any plans the English might have for helping the Emperor against Venice and France. It was quite obvious to him that the Emperor's representative might set the machinery in motion for a fresh assault on war-torn Italy. In particular, he was apprehensive that such a foray would prevent Venice from her rightful possession of the city of

---

[50] L. P., II, 1959; Polydore Vergil, p. 265. It is not possible to determine whether or not Surrey's ejection from the council chamber resulted from his attempt on Wolsey's life. The historian may be dealing with either one or two events. Pollard does not seem to accept Polydore Vergil's story of the attempted stabbing since he does not repeat it. Wolsey, p. 107. However, Pollard implies that there is a connection between Surrey's ouster and his indictment in the king's bench for keeping retainers. Wolsey, of course, as chancellor would be responsible for the rigorous action taken against those who retained. Ibid., p. 76. Surrey's first wife, Anne Plantagenet died at the end of 1512 or beginning of 1513, leaving no issue. He married Elizabeth Stafford, daughter of the Duke of Buckingham, sometime after Easter 1513 and had as issue the famous poet, Henry, Earl of Surrey; Mary Howard, who married the king's natural son, Henry Fitzroy, and another son, Thomas, viscount Bindon, d. 1582. Memorials, pp. 14-15.

[51] C. S. P. Ven., II, 791.

Verona. He tried to point out that any aid given to the Emperor for the purpose of trying to capture Milan from the French would be wasted. After the Venetian ambassador confided his fears to the duke, the latter blandly told the ambassador that the intent of Cardinal Sion's mission was merely to foster world peace. He continued that there was no intent of injuring Venice, but, of course, aid must be given to the Emperor, to whom England was bound by a solemn treaty. Giustinian pressed Norfolk further on this matter, wondering why England would sanction aid to be used against a friendly power, to wit, Venice. Norfolk gruffly reiterated his point about his country's confederacy with the Emperor and took the liberty of muttering something which was not totally understood by his auditor. Finally, to satisfy the ambassador, he swore by God that nothing was under way and that peace was in the offing. Still not satisfied, the Venetian pointed out to the duke that Christians should unite to fight the menacing Turks and not slaughter each other. Norfolk replied that he wished for little other than peace or that some action be taken against the Turks and added that he would do what he could for them. The ambassador left unconvinced by the promise wrung from the duke, for he remembered how the English had acted previously.[52]

Giustinian had good reason to worry. A league consisting of the Holy Roman Empire, England, and Spain for the defense of the Church was contemplated. In October, he noted a league had been entered into by England and Spain[53] and Cardinal Sion was in England to complete details for the Emperor's entrance into the league. Negotiations dragged on interminably, however, and it was not until July 5, 1517 that the treaty was confirmed by Maximilian, Charles, now ruler of Spain, and Henry. Its ratification took place in the presence of Wolsey, Suffolk, Norfolk, Ruthal, and many other English councillors.[54] The treaty was directed against France and her aims in Italy. Implementation of the league was not rapid, despite Wolsey's proven dislike for the French, and it looked as if there would be no war. This, in fact, is what happened and both countries decided to settle their differences amicably in October 1518. Wolsey, who

---

[52] Sebastian Giustinian, *Four Years At The Court Of Henry VIII*, trans. by Rawdon Brown, 2 vols. (London, 1854), I, pp. 309-11. For a discussion of French aims in Italy and Wolsey's attempts to frustrate them through the use of Maximilian see Pollard, *Wolsey*, pp. 111-15.

[53] *L. P.*, II, 2445.

[54] *Ibid.*, 2486, 3437.

was made papal legate earlier in the year,[55] could boast of the new treaties with France which provided for peace and the marriage of Mary, Henry's only child, with the French dauphin. A committee of Norfolk; Ruthal; Charles, earl of Worcester; Lord Herbert; and Nicholas, Bishop of Ely, worked out the details which included the surrender of Tournai won in 1513, the setting up of a dowry of 330,000 gold crowns, and the making of a treaty for universal peace. Norfolk, along with the Dukes of Buckingham and Suffolk and other councillors, signed the treaty for the English.[56]

One possible reason for delay in the ratification of the Holy League was the evil May Day riot of 1517 in which Norfolk helped to subdue the rioting London apprentices. The cause of the riot was the English artisans' hatred of the foreign tradesmen who the English felt were responsible for their own commercially depressed condition. As always, in times of want, it is easy to blame the foreigner, the one who is different, for one's own ills. Incendiary speeches by several priests incited the artisans to talk about the use of violence. Though the authorities had information about the proposed uprising and issued stern warnings to those who might take part in it, one occurred. Norfolk's son Surrey bore the brunt of restoring order, while the duke, the Earl of Shrewsbury, Thomas Docwra, and George Neville closed off all escape routes as the apprentices fled before Surrey[57] ". . . like sheep at the sight of a wolf . . .".[58] The ringleader, John Lincoln, and thirteen of his associates were executed and four hundred persons who had been arrested were granted clemency by Henry after having been made to parade through the city of London wearing rope halters about their necks. Since none of the prisoners knew what his fate would be until he came into Henry's presence at Westminster Hall,[59] Henry was able to make them feel the power which a king has over his subjects and also gratefulness to their merciful sovereign.

During the year 1519 Maximilian, the Holy Roman Emperor, died. Since his office was elective, rumours were rife as to who his successor would be. Although the logical choice was Charles, the king of Spain, both Francis I and Henry VIII entertained some slight hopes of gaining the coveted crown. The fact that they seriously sought this prize, a symbol of the Christian unity of western Europe and the

---

[55] Pollard, *Wolsey*, p. 116.
[56] *L. P.*, II, 4467, 4468, 4469.
[57] Polydore Vergil, pp. 243-45. Mackie, p. 298.
[58] Polydore Vergil, p. 245.
[59] Mackie, p. 298.

theoretical temporal power of the Christian world, indicated that the world they lived in was still dominated by medieval conceptions. Their minds fastened on the medieval, they looked to the past: why else would Francis I try to dominate the Italian city states, if not to control the seat of ancient Roman power; or Henry VIII defend the church against Luther; or both of them dream that the King of the Romans' crown was within their grasp? If they could not get it for themselves, perhaps they could see that Charles did not obtain it. It is not surprising, then, that Norfolk's considered opinion expressed to the Venetian ambassador was that neither Charles nor Francis would get the crown, but one of the German princes, since Henry had taken action to insure free elections.[60]

Norfolk's position as one of the executive committee running England's administration and his interest and influence in diplomacy made him one of the three or four most important men in the realm. Sebastian Giustinian listed him as one of the possible successors to the English throne should Henry die without male heirs. Admittedly, his chances were not as good as the popular Edward Stafford, duke of Buckingham, who had an income of 30,000 ducats (£11,250), nor of Charles Brandon, the duke of Suffolk, who had an income of 12,000 ducats (£4,500) and high hopes for the throne through the right of his wife Mary, but Norfolk's income was a respectable 12,000 ducats and he was on excellent terms with Wolsey.[61] The possibility of the king dying without a male heir was a serious problem by 1519 in view of Catherine's advancing age. The birth of Princess Mary in 1516, far from disappointing Henry, emboldened him to hope for a male heir and he remarked to Giustinian at Princess Mary's christening: "We are both young; if it was a daughter this time, by the grace of God the sons will follow. . . ."[62] But in his heart he must have known

---

[60] C. S. P. Ven., II, 1220.
[61] Ibid., 1287. The Venetian ambassador's estimate of Buckingham's revenue seems excessive in the light of Pollard's figure of £6045. There is great difficulty in attempting to assess Norfolk's worth since we do not have an I.P.M. for him or his stepmother or a complete one for his father; nor is there one for the dowager Duchess of Norfolk whose property Thomas inherited. Perhaps we can better estimate his worth when historians gain access to the muniments at Arundel Castle. However, the Venetian figure of 12,000 ducats or £4,500 may not be far off since his debts and moveable goods in Suffolk were estimated for the subsidy of 1524 at more than £4000, then being worth more than his lands. Julian Cornwall, ed., The Lay Subsidy Rolls For The County Of Sussex (= Sussex Record Society, LVI) (Lewes, Sussex, 1957), p. 1. Pollard, Wolsey, p. 322.
[62] L. P., II, 1585.

that Catherine was not going to do the one thing she must do if she were to be a successful queen. Henry needed an heir desperately. As early as 1514 the expedient of repudiation of Catherine was suggested to him and preliminary work done with this in view.[63] Henry's conscience became more tender with each passing year, but he did not cast Catherine aside. The problem of the influential subject in a situation where the king lacked male heirs was a ticklish one, and Henry was extremely sensitive to it. He did not need to worry much about Norfolk: the duke had learned his lesson years earlier and never gave the king cause for concern. Henry could entrust his kingdom to Norfolk, as he did when he and Catherine went to meet Francis in 1520 at the Field of the Cloth of Gold, and feel satisfied that the duke would perform his duties and no more. The king expected and received a letter from the duke informing him that his daughter was well and that the kingdom's affairs were in order.[64]

Neither the king nor Wolsey, however, were sure of the affection and loyalty of the Duke of Buckingham, the Earl of Surrey's father-in-law. Rumours of his chances for the throne and Surrey's forcible ejection from the council chamber in 1516 made both men suspect, especially by Wolsey. Wolsey nursed his grudge against the two men and carefully constructed a case of treason against Buckingham. First, Wolsey arranged for Surrey's nomination as Lieutenant of Ireland which effectively removed the earl from the sphere of English politics, and the possibility that he would interfere with Wolsey's case against Buckingham.[65] Then, Buckingham was summoned to London during the first part of April 1521 and on April 16 was arrested for treason. On May 11 Norfolk was appointed high steward for the trial which occurred on the thirteenth. As the sentence of guilty was pronounced, Norfolk wept unashamedly. At eleven o'clock on May 17 Buckingham was beheaded.[66] Despite his friendship for Buckingham, Norfolk quite willingly accepted a royal grant of some of Buckingham's property.[67]

---

[63] Betty Behrens, "A Note On Henry VIII's Divorce Project Of 1514", *Bull. Instit. Hist. Research*, XI (1933-34), pp. 163-64. See also *C. S. P. Ven.*, II, 479 which cites the rumor that Henry planned to repudiate Catherine and marry a daughter of the French Duke of Bourbon.

[64] *L. P.*, III, 873.

[65] Polydore Vergil, p. 265.

[66] L. W. Vernon Harcourt, *His Grace The Steward And Trial of Peers...* (London, 1907), pp. 435-41. For a full account of Buckingham's trial see *L. P.*, "Introduction", III, cxxvi-cxxxvii.

[67] *J. H. L.*, I, xvi, xlv, cxvi.

Buckingham's real crime was not in listening to prophecies of the king's death and of his own succession to the throne, which was alleged at his trial,[68] but in having been born too close to the throne. As was previously mentioned, his descent from Edward III made him a likely candidate for the crown should Henry die without heirs. Should the king die, leaving his young daughter Mary to succeed him, the prospect of a protectorship was exhilarating. The memory of Richard III still lingered on, if not in the mind of the young king, at least in the minds of other older men who had seen far more troubled times. The last Yorkist king's career presented a political lesson to both noblemen and king. That is why the Tudor monarchs, always sensitive to the succession question, made it a practice of eliminating possible contenders for the royal sceptre. Henry VII had no scruples about executing the young Earl of Warwick, the Duke of Clarence's son, whose claim to the throne was better, from a Yorkist point of view, than his own. Nor could Henry VIII permit the existence of a rival claimant, especially if that man compounded the curse of royal blood with an over-active imagination. Buckingham's position as first duke in the realm and as the wealthiest nobleman to boot made him dangerous. Mere gossip about his chances of succeeding Henry was enough to indict him in the eyes of the crown. Wolsey, that jealous guardian of the crown's prerogative, was quick to take Henry aside and point out that Buckingham posed a very real threat.[69] Whether or not Buckingham actively sought the purple did not matter; he represented in his person the possibility or potentiality for so doing, and for Henry, this was sufficient reason for his condemnation. Thus, Buckingham, as many sixteenth-century men, died a convicted traitor, but still died as he maintained, the king's true subject. The power of the crown had been exalted and an object lesson administered to the nobility.

In December 1522, Norfolk resigned as treasurer with his son Thomas taking his place,[70] and in 1523 he made his last important public appearance when he was present at the opening of parliament where he was a trier of petitions of England, Ireland, Wales, and

---

[68] *D. N. B.*, XVIII, 855.
[69] Pollard, *Wolsey*, p. 100.
[70] Surrey was granted the office of Treasurer of the Exchequer on December 4 and he received the same wage his father did, twenty shillings a day. *L. P.*, III, 2700; *L. P.*, XXI, 556. But Norfolk's office as earl marshal was not given to his son Surrey, but reserved for the Duke of Suffolk who received the reversion of the office on July 4, 1523. *L. P.*, III, 3161.

Scotland as he had been in 1510, 1512, and 1515.[71] From the time of his creation as a duke until his retirement as treasurer, Norfolk was most busy as a diplomat and councillor. Although he proved unequal to managing Henry and his council, he was an important minister whose advice was listened to and sometimes followed. His policy of friendship with France was ultimately adopted by Wolsey, at least in 1518. Of course, whether Wolsey accepted this policy at Norfolk's urging is another matter, and in most cases the duke deferred to the chancellor. Wolsey's authority in the council was supreme. He ordered literally everything. For example, when Norfolk's son Surrey sought his father's post as treasurer, Henry told the earl to ask Wolsey for it.[72] And when Norfolk was regent of England during Henry's absence in

[71] *C. S. P. Ven.*, III, 663. Little is known about the duties of triers of petitions. One of the funcitons of parliament was to hear petitions of English subjects and to take any action deemed necessary. Since the fully convened parliament could not take the time to hear all petitions individually, much of this work was undoubtedly done by committees, hence the Receivers of Petitions for England, Ireland, and Wales, the Triers of Petitions for the same, the Receivers of Petitions for Gascony and lands and countries beyond the seas and isles, and the Triers of Petition for Gascony, etc. Probably the receivers of petitions received, sorted, and recorded the petitions presented to them, and then passed them on to the triers of petitions who tried the petitions in the judicial sense. Pollard has suggested that the relationship between the receivers and triers was something akin to that of a clerk to a judge. The receivers were compelled by the triers to tell whatever they knew of each petitioner and his petition, and also acted as messengers from the Lords to the Commons. Actions taken on individual petitions varied from granting the petition, requesting amendment, and referring it to any one of a number of the king's officials. *Journals Of The House Of Lords*, I, lxxvi, 4, 10, 18; A. F. Pollard, "Receivers of Petitions and Clerks of Parliament," *E. H. R.*, LVII (1942), 202-13. For the origin of parliamentary petitions see Pollard, *Parliament*, p. 37. Associated with Norfolk as triers of petitions in 1510 were Warham, the Duke of Buckingham, Fox, the Bishop of Exeter and of Rochester, the Earl of Shrewsbury, the Abbots of Bury St. Edmunds and Abyndon, and Lord Herbert and Lord Hastings. There were six prelates, including Warham, the chancellor, and five lords, including Norfolk, the treasurer. They were to execute their office together or with a quorum of at least five of the lords and prelates and were to call the treasurer and chancellor or two other officers of the king to them as necessary. *J. H. L.*, I, 4. Similarly the triers of petitions for Gascony were empowered to call when necessary the sergeant of the king, the chamberlain, and the treasurer, but in 1515 this was changed. They no longer could call the chamberlain or treasurer, but they could call the king's sergeants and solicitor. They still met in the treasurer's chamber. *Ibid.*, I, 10, 19. The calling of the treasurer and chancellor notes an additional duty of treasurer and, perhaps brings to mind, administrative and judicial duties of the executive council of chancellor, treasurer, and privy seal. Norfolk was a receiver of petitions for England, Ireland, and Wales in 1515 and 1523. *Ibid.*, I, lxxvi, 18.
[72] *L. P. Addenda*, I, 356.

1520, he would not allow Thomas, lord Darcy, to sit in Princess Mary's council because Wolsey wished Darcy to remain in the country.[73] Though he never became the king's first minister, Norfolk did perform valuable service to the crown and his retirement from active political life marked an end to over fifty years of public employment.

[73]   *Ibid.*, 286.

EPILOGUE

After retiring from public life, Norfolk left court and took up residence at his ducal seat, Framlingham Castle in Suffolk. His son Surrey's chief dwelling, Tendring Hall, in Stoke Nayland, Suffolk, was not too far distant and during the last year of his life the eighty year old duke visited his son's family at Tendring Hall on August 5 and August 6, 1523. He arrived in time for supper on Wednesday the fifth. His company included his wife Agnes and their children Anne, Elizabeth, and another son named Thomas. The company dined in the Countess of Surrey's chamber since her husband, the earl, was off on the king's business as Lieutenant-General of the North. The countess served her guests lavishly with two courses which included chicken, mutton, beef, capons, rabbit, pigeons, partridge, quail, venison pasties, and a tart. For breakfast the next morning the duke and duchess were each content with a boiled capon and a piece of beef, while the duke's grandson, the six year old Henry Howard, better known as the famous poet, Earl of Surrey, had a breast of mutton and a chicken. The company stayed the better part of Thursday, had another glorious repast at dinner, and left before supper.[1]

The duke did not long enjoy his retirement from public life or a pleasant country existence, for he died in May 1524. Before death he requested that £133 6s 8d be allowed for the making of effigies of himself and his wife Agnes for his tomb.[2] His body was laid in the castle chapel and the choir draped with black cloth. Three masses

---

[1] California Ms. Ac. 523 fols. 69 (r & v), 70 (r). I am grateful to the University of California at Berkeley for permission to use this document.
[2] Francis Blomefield, An Essay Towards A Topographical History Of The County Of Norfolk . . . , 11 vols. (London, 1805-10), II, 119-20. There is dispute about the date of his death. A Latin account found in Butley Abbey records it as May 18, 1524, but the more generally accepted date is May 21, 1524, which Blomefield uses. A. Leigh Hunt, The Capital Of The Ancient Kingdom Of East Anglia (London, 1870), p. 374. Hereafter cited as Hunt.

daily were said for the soul of the departed duke and each night twelve gentlemen, twelve yeomen, two gentlemen ushers, and two yeomen ushers kept watch. On the twenty-second of June his body was removed from the castle to be interred at Thetford. The richly arrayed corpse was placed in a horse-drawn chariot and taken to Thetford in a long procession of knights, gentlemen, and friars accompanied by four hundred men wearing hooded gowns and bearing brightly lit torches.[3] When the body had been honorably received at Thetford Abbey, the prior celebrated mass at St. Mary's church and the Cistercian Dr. Makerell preached on the subject "Behold, the lion of the tribe of Judah triumphs."[4]

As Dr. Makerell preached from his text in *Revelation,* a sudden fear came over the congregation, and they became so frightened by the priest's words that they ran out of the church, leaving the priest standing all alone.[5] Apparently no further incident occurred that day, for the service was completed and personal officers of Norfolk's household ended the ceremony at the graveside by breaking the ensigns of their office and casting them into the grave.[6] Thus, was the Duke of Norfolk honorably interred with all the dignity due his rank.

At his death, the duke had a reputation as the most famous general in the realm, and his son and namesake, Thomas, the earl of Surrey, was following in his father's footsteps as Henry VIII's most active general. Not unnaturally, the duke developed his professional interest in military tactics and strategy into a private avocation. Three years before his death, he requested that Alexander Barclay translate into English, Sallust's *Bellum Jugurthinum.* Besides his keen interest in military matters, the duke was distressed by his countrymen's lack of interest in the French language, and he was quite pleased to accept Barclay's dedication of a work which was described as an introduction to the writing and pronunciation of French.[7] His concern with French when most scholars were mastering Greek and polishing up their classical Latin, marks the duke as a member of the generation which antedated the new learning. Little did the duke know that the foundations of his world were soon to crumble.

---

[3] Thomas Martin, *The History Of The Town Of Thetford In The Counties Of Norfolk And Suffolk, From The Earliest Accounts To The Present Time* (London, 1779), Appendix, p. 38.

[4] Hunt, pp. 374-75.

[5] Martin, pp. 122-23.

[6] Hunt, p. 374.

[7] *D. N. B.,* III, 157.

Aside from his military and conciliar career, Norfolk's most enduring achievement can be found in his progeny. The duke left three children by his first wife: Thomas, the heir to the dukedom and his estates; Lord Edmund Howard, the father of the ill-fated Catherine, fifth wife to Henry VIII; and Elizabeth Howard, wife to Thomas Boleyn, viscount Rochford, and mother of Ann Boleyn, Henry VIII's second wife.

By his second wife he left: Lord William Howard, founder of the Effingham branch of the Howards and Lord Admiral under Queen Mary; a second Thomas Howard, who died in 1537 for treasonously aspiring to marry Margaret Douglas, daughter of Margaret Tudor and her second husband, the Earl of Angus; Lady Ann married to John de Vere, fourteenth earl of Oxford; Lady Catherine who married the heir of Sir Rice ap Thomas of Wales; Lady Elizabeth who married Henry Radcliffe, baron Fitzwalter and later earl of Sussex; and Lady Dorothy, not then married but who later married Edward Stanley, the earl of Derby.[8] The listing of Norfolk's children and their marriages reads like a directory of the most important of sixteenth-century English nobility. Two of the duke's granddaughters married Henry VIII; another married Henry's natural son, Henry Fitz-roy. Most of the duke's daughters married important nobles. The granddaughters who were fortunate enough to marry Henry were not fortunate enough to keep their heads. Even Norfolk's son and heir, Thomas, spent six years in the Tower from 1547 to 1553, and his grandson, the celebrated Earl of Surrey, lost his head in 1547 for quartering the arms of England, and his great-grandson, the fourth duke, lost his head in 1572 for attempting to marry Mary, Queen of Scots. The sixteenth-century history of the ubiquitous, conniving Howards is an exciting one, which it must be remembered was built on the solid foundations laid by the second Duke of Norfolk.

At death, Norfolk owed not a groat to any man.[9] He had creditably performed whatever duty was assigned him and in the process of his long life endeared himself to no less than four different English sovereigns. His eighty odd years were filled with various services performed for each king, though he will be especially remembered as Richard III's steward, as Henry VII's Lieutenant of the North, and as Henry VII and Henry VIII's Treasurer General. A gruff man on occasion, he knew how to adapt himself to please the king of his age,

---

[8] Weever, pp. 839-40; *Memorials*, pp. 8, 11-12, 87-88.
[9] Weever, p. 839.

though his experiences with their queens was something less than successful. He was a man's man. And in his prime he might have been able to say as Kent, the faithful follower of King Lear:

I can keep honest counsel, ride, run, mar a curious tale in telling it, and deliver a plain message bluntly. That which ordinary men are fit for, I am qualified in; and the best of me is diligence.[10]

10   Shakespeare, p. 1146.

LIST OF MANUSCRIPTS AND WORKS CITED

MANUSCRIPTS

Bodleian Ashmole Ms. 841. A new patent for the earldom of Surrey, 1492.

B. M. Additional 19152. Tylney Pedigree.

B. M. Additional Charter 16559. Account of John Penley, receiver of John Howard for various lordships in Cambridge, Essex, Hertford, Norfolk, and Suffolk.

B. M. Egerton 2603. Warrant for payment of the fee of the crown, 1505.

B. M. Harley 433. Grants made by Richard III.

B. M. Sloane 1523. Sayings of famous Tudors.

Calendar Of The Close Rolls Preserved In The Public Record Office. Unpublished manuscript of Vol. II for Henry VII, kept in the Round Room at the P. R. O.

California Ms. Ac. 523. The Catorer's Book Of The Household Of Thomas Howard, Earl Of Surrey, For 17 April 1523 to 18 January 1524.

Essex Record Office D/Dpr/139. Compotus of Clement Heigham, receiver general of John de Vere, earl of Oxford, for the year 1488-1489.

Huntington Library Ms. El. 2655. The Ellesmere Extracts from the 'Acta Consilii' of King Henry VIII.

P.R.O. C66/569, 570, 576. Patents of Henry VII.

P.R.O. C71/107. Scottish Roll for 4 H VII to 8 H VII.

P.R.O. C82/60. A patent of Henry VII.

P.R.O. DL 29/10512, 10513, 10514, 10515, 10516. Ministers Accounts for the royal lordship of Sheriff Hutton, 5 H VII to 8 H VII.

P.R.O. E405/60, 61. Tellers Rolls for 15 Edward IV.

P.R.O. E405(2)/75, 76, 77, 78, 79, 80, 81. Tellers Rolls for 1 H VII to 20 H VII.

P.R.O. E405/82, 83, 84, 85, 86. Tellers Rolls for 24 H VII to 4 H VIII.

York House Books, volume VII for 1490-1496.

PRINTED PRIMARY SOURCES

Allen, P. S. and H. M. (eds.), *Letters Of Richard Fox, 1486-1527* (Oxford, 1929).

Barnard, Francis Pierrepont (ed.), *Edward IV's French Expedition of 1475: The Leaders and Their Badges being MS. 2. M. 16 College of Arms* (Oxford, 1925).

Batten, Edmund C., ed., *The Register of Richard Fox, While Bishop of Bath and Wells, A. D. MCCCCXCII-MCCCCXCIV* (London, 1889).

Bayne, C. G., and Dunham, William Huse, Jr. (eds.), *Select Cases In The Council Of Henry VII* (= *Selden Society*, Vol. 75) (London, 1958).

Calendar Of The Close Rolls Preserved In The Public Record Office. Edward IV-Henry VII, 4 vols. (London, 1949, 1953, 1954, 1955).

Calendar Of Documents Relating To Scotland Preserved In Her Majesty's Public Record Office, 4 vols. (Edinburgh, 1881-1888).

Calendar Of Inquisitions Post Mortem And Other Analogous Documents Preserved In The Public Record Office — Henry VII, 3 vols. (London, 1898, 1915, 1955).

Calendar Of The Patent Rolls Preserved In The Public Record Office. Henry VI-Henry VII, 6 vols. (London, 1897-1916).

Calendar of Letters, Despatches, and State Papers Relating To Negotiations Between England And Spain Preserved In The Archives At Simancas And Elsewhere, ed. by G. A. Bergenroth, *et al.*, 13 vols. (London, 1862-1954).

Calendar Of State Papers And Manuscripts Existing In The Archives And Collections Of Milan, ed. by A. B. Hinds (London, 1912).

Calendar Of State Papers And Manuscripts, Relating To English Affairs, Existing In The Archives And Collections Of Venice, And In Other Libraries Of Northern Italy, ed. by Rawdon Brown, *et al.*, 38 vols. (London, 1864-1947).

Camden, William, *Remains Of A Greater Work Concerning Britaine* (London, 1605).

Campbell, Mildred (ed.), *The Utopia Of Sir Thomas More including Roper's Life Of More And His Daughter Margaret* (New York, 1947).

Campbell, William (ed.), *Materials For A History Of The Reign Of Henry VII*, 2 vols. (London, 1873-77).

Collier, J. Payne (ed.), *Household Books Of John [Howard], Duke of Norfolk And Thomas, Earl of Surrey: Temp. 1481-90* (London, Roxburghe Club, 1844).

Cornwall, Julian (ed.), *The Lay Subsidy Rolls For The County Of Sussex 1524-25* (= *Sussex Record Society*, LVI) (Lewes, Sussex, 1957).

Dyce, Alexander (ed.), *The Poetical Works Of John Skelton*, 2 vols. (London, 1843).

The Eclogues of Alexander Barclay, ed. by Beatrice While (= E. E. T. S., Orig. Series, No. 175) (London, 1928).

Ellis, Henry, *Original Letters, Illustrative of English History*, 2nd ed. First Series, 3 vols. (London, 1825).

——, *Three Books Of Polydore Vergil's English History, Comprising The Reigns Of Henry VI, Edward IV, And Richard III* (= Camden Society, First Series, XXIX) (London, 1844).

Foedera, Conventiones, Litterae, Et. Cujuscunque Generis Acta Publica, Inter Reges Angliae, Et Alios quosvis Imperatores, Reges, Pontifices, Principes, vel Communitates, ed. by Thomas Rymer. 2nd ed. by George Holmes, 20 vols. (London, 1727-35).

Gairdner, James (ed.), *Historia Regis Henrici Septimi, A Bernardo Andrea Tholosota Conscripta: Necnon Alia Quaedam Ad Eundem Regem Spectantia* (London, 1858).

——, *The Paston Letters A. D. 1422-1509*, New ed., 6 vols. (London, 1904).

——, *Three Fifteenth Century Chronicles* (= Camden Society, New Series, XXVIII) (London, 1880).

Garrett, William (ed.), *The Battle Of Flodden Field* (Newcastle, 1822).

Giustinian, Sebastian, *Four Years At The Court Of Henry VIII*, trans. by Rawdon Brown, 2 vols. (London, 1854).

Grosart, Alexander B. (ed.), *The Poems Of Sir John Beaumont, Bart* (Beachburn, Lancashire, 1869).

Hall, Edward, *Henry VIII*, ed. by Charles Whibley, 2 vols. (London, 1904).

Hall's Chronicle; Containing The History Of England, During The Reign Of Henry The Fourth, And The Succeeding Monarchs, To The End Of The

Reign Of Henry The Eighth, In Which Are Particularly Described The Manners And Customs Of Those Periods, ed. by Henry Ellis (London, 1809).

Hay, Denys (ed. and trans.), *The Anglica Historia Of Polydore Vergil A. D. 1485-1537* (= *Camden Society, New Series, LXXIV*) (London, 1950).

Howard, Henry, *Indication of Memorials, Monuments, Paintings, and Engravings of Persons of the Howard Family, and of their Wives and Children, and of those who have married Ladies of the Name, and of the Representatives of some of its Branches now extinct; as far as they have been ascertained* (Corbey Castle, 1834).

Journals Of The House Of Lords, Beginning Anno Primo Henrici Octavi. 10 vols. (London, 1846).

Kingsford, Charles L. (ed.), *Chronicles of London* (Oxford, 1905).

Leland, John, *Antiquarii De Rebvs Brittannicis Collectanea*, 2nd ed. 6 vols. (London, 1770).

Letters And Papers, Foreign And Domestic Of The Reign Of Henry VIII, 1509-1547, ed. by J. S. Brewer, J. Gairdner, and R. H. Brodie, 21 vols. and a volume of addenda (London, 1862-1932).

Letters And Papers Illustrative Of The Reigns Of Richard III. And Henry VII, ed. by James Gairdner, 2 vols. (London, 1861-63).

Lindesay, Robert, *The Historie and Cronicles of Scotland*, ed. by A. E. J. G. MacKay, 3 vols. (Edinburgh-London, 1899-1911).

Macpherson, D.; Caley, J.; Illingworth, W.; Horne, T. H., *Rotuli Scotiae In Turri Londiniensi Et In Domo Capitulari Westmonasteriensi Asservati (1291-1516)*, 2 vols. (London, 1814-19).

Madox, Thomas, *Formulare Anglicanum* (London, 1702).

Malden, Henry Elliot (ed.), *The Cely Papers: Selections From The Correspondence And Memoranda Of The Cely Family, Merchants Of The Staple A.D. 1475-1488* (= *Camden Society, Third Series, I*) (London, 1900).

The Manuscripts of the Corporations of Southampton and King's Lynn (London, Historical Manuscripts Commission, 1887).

Myers, A. R. (ed.), *The Household Of Edward IV: The Black Book And The Ordinance Of 1478* (Manchester, 1959).

Nicolas, Nicholas Harris, *Testamenta Vetusta: Being Illustrations From Wills Of Manners Customs &c*, 2 vols. (London, 1826).

Oppenheim, M., *Naval Accounts and Inventories Of The Reign Of Henry VII 1485-8 And 1495-9* (= *Publications Of The Navy Records Society, VIII*) (London, 1896).

The Poems Of Henry Howard, Earl Of Surrey (London, n. d.).

Pollard, A. F. (ed.), *The Reign Of Henry VII From Contemporary Sources*, 3 vols. (London, 1913-14).

Raine, Angelo (ed.), *York Civic Records*, 8 vols., XCVIII, CIII, CVI, CVIII, CX, CXII, CXV, CXIX (Wakefield, The Yorkshire Archaeological Society, 1939-52).

Raine, James and James, Jr. (eds.), *Testamenta Eboracensia Or Wills Registered at York Illustrative Of The History, Manners, Language, Statistics, &c. Of The Province Of York From The Year MCCC Downwards*, 6 vols. (London, Surtees Society, 1836-1902).

Rastell, William (ed.), *The workes of Sir Thomas More Knyght, sometyme Lorde Chauncellour of England, wrytten by him in the Englysh tonge* (London, 1557).

Rotuli Parliamentorum: Vt Et Petitiones Et Placita In Parliamento (1278-1504). 6 vols. (n.p., n.d.).

Smith, G. Gregory (ed.), *The Days Of James IIII, 1488-1513* (London, 1900).

Stapleton, Thomas (ed.), *Plumpton Correspondence: A Series Of Letters, Chiefly Domestick, Written In The Reigns Of Edward IV, Richard III, Henry VII, And Henry VIII* (= Camden Society, First Series, IV) (London, 1839).

Steele, Robert, *A Bibliography Of Royal Proclamations Of The Tudor And Stuart Sovereigns And Of Others Published Under Authority 1485-1714 With An Historical Essay On Their Origin And Use*, 2 vols. (Oxford, 1910).

Thomas, A. H., and Thornley, I. D. (eds.), *The Great Chronicle of London* (London, 1938).

Turner, Thomas Hudson (ed.), *Manners And Household Expenses Of England In The Thirteenth And Fifteenth Centuries Illustrated By Original Records* (London, Roxburghe Club, 1841).

Visitations of Suffolk 1561, 1577, 1612, ed. by W. G. Metcalfe (Exeter, 1882).

Weever, John, *Ancient Fvnerall Monuments Within The vnited Monarchie of Great Britaine, Ireland, and The Islands adiacent, with the dissolved Monasteries therein contained; their Founders, and what eminent persons have beene in the same interred* (London, 1631).

SECONDARY WORKS

Allen, Thomas, *A New And Complete History Of The County of York*, 3 vols. (London, 1828-31).

Atton, Henry, and Holland, Henry Hurst, *The King's Customs*, 2 vols. (London, 1908-10).

Austin, Alfred, *Flodden Field: A Tragedy* (New York, 1903).

Bacon, Francis, *Essays, Advancement Of Learning, New Atlantis, And Other Pieces*, ed. by Richard Foster Jones (New York, 1937).

Bindoff, S. T., *Tudor England* (Harmondsworth, Middlesex, 1950).

Blomefield, Francis, *An Essay Towards A Topographical History Of The County Of Norfolk*, 11 vols. (London, 1805-10).

Brenan, Gerald, and Statham, Edward Phillips, *The House of Howard*, 2 vols. (New York, 1908).

Burke's Genealogical And Heraldic History Of The Peerage Baronetage and Knightage, ed. by L. G. Pine, 102nd ed. (London, 1959).

Cokayne, G. E., *The Complete Peerage*, ed. by V. Gibbs, *et. al.*, 13 vols. (London, 1910-59).

Collins, Arthur, *The Peerage Of England Containing A Genealogical and Historical Account Of All the Peers of England, Now Existing Either by Tenure, Summons, or Creation*, 2nd ed., 5 vols. (London, 1741-56).

Creighton, Mandell, *Cardinal Wolsey* (London, 1888).

Dallaway, James, and Cartwright, Edmund, *A History Of The Western Division Of The County Of Sussex, Including The Rapes Of Chichester, Arundel, and Bramber, With The City And Diocese of Chichester*, 2 vols. (London, 1815-32).

Devey, Joseph (ed.), *The Moral and Historical Works Of Lord Bacon, Including His Essays, Apophthegms, Wisdom Of The Ancients, New Atlantis And Life Of Henry The Seventh* (London, 1852).

The Dictionary Of National Biography, ed. by Leslie Stephen and Sidney Lee. Reprint, 22 vols. (London, 1949-50).

Dietz, Frederick C., *English Government Finance, 1485-1558* (= University of Illinois Studies In The Social Sciences, IX, no. 3) (Urbana, Ill., 1921).

Edwards, J. G., Galbraith, V. H., and Jacob, E. F. (eds.), *Historical Essays In Honour Of James Tait* (Manchester, 1933).

Elton, G. R., *The Tudor Revolution In Government: Administrative Changes In The Reign Of Henry VIII* (Cambridge, 1953).

Ferguson, Charles W., *Naked To Mine Enemies: The Life of Cardinal Wolsey* (Boston, 1958).

Gairdner, James, *Henry The Seventh* (London, 1892).

——, *History Of The Life And Reign Of Richard III*, New ed. (Cambridge, 1898).

——, *The Houses of Lancaster And York With The Conquest And Loss of France* (New York, 1875).

Green, Mary A. E., *Lives Of The Princesses Of England From The Norman Conquest*, 6 vols. (London, 1857).

Green, R., *The History, Topography, And Antiquities Of Framlangham And Saxsted, In The County Of Suffolk, From The Earliest Period To The Present Time* (London, 1834).

Harcourt, L. W. Vernon, *His Grace The Steward And Trial Of Peers: A Novel Inquiry Into a Special Branch Of Constitutional Government* (London, 1907).

Harvey, John, *English Medieval Architects: A Biographical Dictionary Down To 1550 Including Master Masons, Carpenters, Building Contractors and others responsible for Design* (London, 1954).

Herbert, Lord Edward of Cherbury, *The History Of England Under Henry VIII* (London, 1870).

Hunt, A. Leigh, *The Capital Of The Ancient Kingdom Of East Anglia* (London, 1870).

Hutchinson, William, *The History and Antiquities Of The County Palatine of Durham*, 3 vols. (Newcastle, 1785-94).

Kendall, Paul Murray, *Richard The Third* (London, 1955).

Kingsford, C. L., *Prejudice & Promise in XVth Century England* (Oxford, 1925).

Lamb, V. B., *The Betrayal Of Richard III* (London, 1959).

Leather, Gerald F. T., *New Light On Flodden*, 2nd ed. (Berwick, 1938).

LeStrange, Hamon, *Norfolk Official Lists* (Norwich, 1890).

Mackenzie, W. M., *The Secret of Flodden With 'The Rout of the Scots'* (Edinburgh, 1931).

Mackie, J. D., *The Earlier Tudors 1485-1558* (Oxford, 1957).

Mackie, R. L., *King James IV Of Scotland: A Brief Survey of His Life and Times* (London, 1958).

Manning, Owen, and Bray, William, *The History And Antiquities Of The County Of Surrey: Compiled From The Best And Most Authentic Historians, Valuable Records, And Manuscripts In The Public Offices and Libraries, And In Private Hands*, 3 vols. (London, 1804-14).

Martin, Thomas, *The History Of The Town Of Thetford In The Counties Of Norfolk And Suffolk, From The Earliest Accounts To The Present Time* (London, 1779).

Mattingly, Garrett, *Catherine Of Aragon* (Boston, 1941).

——, *Renaissance Diplomacy* (Boston, 1955).

Metcalfe, Walter C., *A Book Of Knights Banneret, Knights of the Bath, and Knights Bachelor Made Between the Fourth Year Of King Henry VI And The Restoration Of King Charles II* (London, 1885).

Mills, Charles, *The History of Chivalry or Knighthood and its times* (London, 1826).

Morant, Philip, *The History And Antiquities Of The County Of Essex*. Reprint, 2 vols. (Chelmsford, 1816).

Neilson, William Allan, and Hill, Charles Jarvis (eds.), *The Complete Plays and Poems of William Shakespeare* (New York, 1942).

A New English Dictionary On Historical Principles, ed. by James A. H. Murray, et al., 10 vols. (Oxford, 1888-1928).

Oman, Charles, *A History Of The Art Of War In The Sixteenth Century* (London, 1937).

——, *The History Of England From The Accession Of Richard II. To The Death Of Richard III.* (1377-1485) (London, 1906).

Pegge, Samuel, *Curialia: Or An Historical Account Of Some Branches Of The Royal Household, &c. &c.*, 2 vols. (London, 1791-1806).

Pollard, A. F., *The Evolution Of Parliament*, 2nd ed. (London, 1926).

——, *Wolsey*, New ed. (London, 1953).

Power, Eileen, and Postan, M. M. (eds.), *Studies In English Trade In The Fifteenth Century* (London, 1933).

Ramsay, James H., *Lancaster And York: A Century Of English History (A.D. 1399-1485)*, 2 vols. (Oxford, 1892).

Reid, R. R., *The King's Council In The North* (London, 1921).

Richardson, W. C., *Tudor Chamber Administration, 1485-1547* (Baton Rouge, La., 1952).

Ridpath, George, *The Border History Of England And Scotland*. Revised by Philip Ridpath (Berwick, 1848).

Round, J. Horace, *Studies In Peerage And Family History* (Westminster, 1901).

Scofield, Cora L., *The Life And Reign Of Edward The Fourth King of England and of France and Lord of Ireland*, 2 vols. (London, 1923).

Smith, Lacey Baldwin, *A Tudor Tragedy: The Life and Times of Catherine Howard* (London, 1961).

Smyth, John, *The Berkeley Manuscripts: The Lives of the Berkeleys Lords Of The Honour, Castle And Manor Of Berkeley In The County of Gloucester From 1066 to 1618*, ed. by Sir John Mac Clean, 3 vols. (Gloucester, 1883-1885).

Stahlman, W. D., and Owen Gingerich, *Solar And Planetary Longitudes For Years −2500 to 2000 by 10-Day Intervals* (Madison, Wis., 1963).

Stubbs, William, *The Constitutional History Of England In Its Origin And Development*, 5th ed., 3 vols. (London, 1896).

Temperley, Gladys, *Henry VII* (Boston-New York, 1914).

Todd, George, *Castellum Huttonicum: Some Account Of Sheriff-Hutton Castle* (York, 1824).

Trevelyan, G. M., *History Of England*, 3rd ed., 3 vols. (London, 1952).

Tytler, Patrick Fraser, *Life Of King Henry The Eighth*, 2nd ed. (Edinburgh, 1837).

Wedgwood, Josiah C., and Holt, Anne D., *History Of Parliament*, 2 vols. (London, 1936-38).

Wegg, Jervis, *Richard Pace: A Tudor Diplomatist* (London, 1932).

ARTICLES AND PAMPHLETS

Behrens, Bette, "A Note On Henry VIII's Divorce Project Of 1514", *Bull. Inst. Hist. Research*, XI (1933-34), 163-64.

Brooks, F. W., *The Council of the North* (= *Historical Association General Series: G. 25*) (London, 1953).

——, *York And The Council Of The North* (= *St. Anthony's Hall, No. 5*) (London, 1954).

Dunham, William Huse, Jr., "The Ellesmere Extracts from the 'Acta Consilii' of King Henry VIII", *E. H. R.*, LVIII (1943), 301-18.

——, "The Members of Henry VIII's Whole Council, 1509-1527", *E. H. R.*, LIX (1944), 187-210.

——, "Wolsey's Rule Of The King's Whole Council", *A. H. R.*, XLIX (1943-44), 644-62.

Haward, Winifred I., "Economic Aspects of the Wars of the Roses in East Anglia", *E. H. R.*, XL (1926), 170-89.

Kirby, J. L., "The Rise of the Under-Treasurer of the Exchequer", *E. H. R.*, LXXII (1957), 666-77.

McEwen, John, "The Battle Of Flodden, September 9TH, 1513", *History Today*, VIII (1958), 337-46.

Newton, Arthur Percival, "The King's Chamber under the Early Tudors", *E. H. R.*, XXXII (1917), 348-72.

Pollard, A. F., "Receivers of Petitions and Clerks of Parliament", *E. H. R.*, LVII (1942), 202-26.

Williams, C. H., "A Norfolk Parliamentary Election, 1461", *E. H. R.*, XL (1925), 79-86.

"The Yorkshire Rebellion In 1489", *Gents. Mag.*, N.S. XXXVI, pt. 2 (1851), 459-68.

INDEX